# SpringerBriefs in Psychology

## SpringerBriefs in Behavioral Criminology

**Series Editor**

Vincent B. Van Hasselt, Fort Lauderdale, FL, USA

Behavioral Criminology is a multidisciplinary approach that draws on behavioral research for the application of behavioral theories and methods to assessment, prevention, and intervention efforts directed toward violent crime and criminal behavior. Disciplines relevant to this field are criminology; criminal justice (law enforcement and corrections); forensic, correctional, and clinical psychology and psychiatry: neuropsychology, neurobiology, conflict and dispute resolution; sociology, and epidemiology. Areas of study and application include, but are not limited to: specific crimes and perpetrators (e.g., homicide and sex crimes, crimes against children, child exploitation, domestic, school, and workplace violence), topics of current national and international interest and concern (e.g., terrorism and counter terrorism, cyber crime), and strategies geared toward evaluation, identification, and interdiction with regard to criminal acts (e.g., hostage negotiation, criminal investigative analysis, threat and risk assessment). The aim of the proposed Briefs is to provide practitioners and researchers with information, data, and current best practices on important and timely topics in Behavioral Criminology. Each Brief will include a review of relevant research in the area, original data, implications of findings, case illustrations (where relevant), and recommendations for directions that future efforts might take.

More information about this series at http://www.springer.com/series/10850

Jennifer Davidtz • Caroline M. Haskamp
Danielle H. Millen • Brittany Plombon
Giovanna Basilio • Tom D. Kennedy

# Sex Trafficking

## Best practices for assessment and intervention

Springer

Jennifer Davidtz
College of Psychology
Nova Southeastern University
Fort Lauderdale, FL, USA

Caroline M. Haskamp
College of Psychology
Nova Southeastern University
Fort Lauderdale, FL, USA

Danielle H. Millen
College of Psychology
Nova Southeastern University
New York, NY, USA

Brittany Plombon
College of Psychology
Nova Southeastern University
Salt Lake City, UT, USA

Giovanna Basilio
College of Psychology
Nova Southeastern University
Fort Lauderdale, FL, USA

Tom D. Kennedy
College of Psychology
Nova Southeastern University
Fort Lauderdale, FL, USA

ISSN 2192-8363 ISSN 2192-8371 (electronic)
SpringerBriefs in Psychology
ISSN 2194-1866 ISSN 2194-1874 (electronic)
SpringerBriefs in Behavioral Criminolog
ISBN 978-3-031-09119-3 ISBN 978-3-031-09120-9 (eBook)
https://doi.org/10.1007/978-3-031-09120-9



This Springer imprint is published by the registered company Springer Nature Switzerland AG
The registered company address is: Gewerbestrasse 11, 6330 Cham, Switzerland

# Contents

# About the Authors

**Jennifer Davidtz** is an associate professor in the College of Psychology at Nova Southeastern University, where she is also the director of internship training for the Psychology Services Center, and director of Psychological Services for the Emotionally Distressed, a specialty program within the PSC that serves people with serious mental illness and personality disorders. She completed her doctoral training in clinical psychology at the University of Massachusetts Amherst, followed by a doctoral internship at The Harvard Medical School/Cambridge Hospital and post-doctoral fellowship at Harbor-UCLA Medical Center. Dr. Davidtz's clinical and scholarly interests include community psychology, social justice, and the person in context; the treatment of serious mental illness, personality disorders, and complex posttraumatic and dissociative conditions; clinical psychology training and therapist development; contemporary relational psychodynamic approaches to psychotherapy; countertransference and other intersubjective psychotherapy process phenomena; and psychotherapy integration. She also maintains a part-time private practice specializing in the treatment of borderline personality disorder, complex PTSD, and dissociative disorders.

**Caroline M. Haskamp** is a doctoral candidate in the clinical psychology program at Nova Southeastern University (NSU) with a concentration in forensic psychology. Caroline currently holds a master's degree in clinical psychology from NSU. Her primary clinical interests include high-risk and system-involved youth; individuals with serious mental illness including complex trauma and personality disorders; forensic populations; and first responder groups. Her primary research interests are focused on sex trafficking, complex trauma, forensic psychological evaluations, serious mental illness, and crime scene investigators. She has obtained clinical experience working in inpatient behavioral health; outpatient for youth, families, and individuals with serious mental illness; youth and adult diversionary programs; and correctional settings. Caroline has also served as a trainer for law enforcement officers, crime scene investigators, firefighters, and support staff in Crisis Intervention Training, Peer Support Training, and Behavioral Health

Training. In addition, she has participated in international humanitarian travel to provide clinical services to indigenous populations and at-risk youth.

**Danielle H. Millen** is the clinical director of Manhattan CRAN with EAC Network and an adjunct professor for the College of Psychology at Nova Southeastern University. She completed her doctoral training in clinical psychology at Nova Southeastern University, followed by a doctoral internship within the Forensic Track at NYU-Bellevue. Her primary research and clinical interest are focused on assessments and forensic psychology. She currently conducts comprehensive assessments to address the mental health needs of individuals with severe mental illnesses who are reentering New York City from Rikers Island. She has published book chapters and written articles in the areas of juvenile suicidality and crime, psychological assessment, intimate partner violence, and malingering.

**Brittany Plombon** is a forensic postdoctoral fellow at the Utah State Hospital and the Utah Department of Human Services. She completed her doctoral training in clinical psychology (forensic concentration) at Nova Southeastern University, followed by a doctoral internship within the forensic track at the Utah State Hospital. Her primary research and clinical interests are focused on assessments and forensic psychology, individuals with serious mental illness, and first responders. She currently conducts court-ordered forensic evaluations (e.g., competency, violence risk, and criminal responsibility) of inpatient, outpatient, and incarcerated defendants within the Utah criminal justice system. She has served as a presenter and lecturer on behavioral health and peer support training for law enforcement professionals and fire rescue personnel. Lastly, she interned with the FBI as a part of their Honor's Internship Program.

**Giovanna Basilio** is a psychology trainee in the APA accredited clinical PsyD program and forensic concentration at Nova Southeastern University (NSU) in South Florida. She currently holds a Master of Science degree in clinical psychology. Her research interests comprise the impact of potentially traumatic events across immigrant and non-immigrant populations, as well as best practices for the assessment and treatment of US immigrants. She has bilingual (English, Spanish) clinical experience with children, adolescents, adults, and older adults across correctional, community, and healthcare settings. Her trauma and forensic-based training experiences provided her opportunities to develop assessment and intervention skills suitable for individuals of diverse and underserved populations, including minors and adults referred for immigration-related psychological evaluations in Miami-Dade County; children and adolescents residing at a humanitarian community in Ventanilla, Peru; adults detained by Immigration and Customs Enforcement (ICE); as well as Hispanic adult immigrants referred for neuropsychological evaluations or therapy at a neurology institute located in Broward County.

**Tom D. Kennedy** is an associate professor in the College of Psychology at Nova Southeastern University (NSU). He serves as a representative for the NSU IRB and is the site supervisor for the forensic practicum. He received his PhD from the University of Miami. He previously served as an associate professor in the College of Education at NSU where he was co-director of the Applied Research Center and developed and taught multiple courses including methods of inquiry, statistics, advanced statistics, research design, mixed methods, program evaluation, survey and measurement and testing. His clinical experience consists of providing forensic evaluations, neuropsychological assessments, behavioral medicine interventions, and child and adolescent therapy in inpatient and outpatient settings including the University of Texas Southwestern Medical Center, UM Mailman Center for Child Development, Jackson Memorial Hospital, UM Institute for Individual and Family Therapy, and the Dallas County Jail. Before coming to NSU, he spent 5 years at the Mailman Center for Child Development, where he trained and supervised school psychologists and assessed children throughout Miami-Dade County Schools. He is board certified in biofeedback. His research interests include three convergent forensic tracks, one focused on at-risk children and adolescents, the other on domestic violence and human trafficking, and a third on the reliability and validity of psychological instruments used in forensic evaluations. He has procured grant funding and served as lead evaluator for multiple organizations including Catholic Charities, Miami Dade-Schools Police, and national bullying programs. He has published books and book chapters, and written articles in the areas of juvenile crime, psychological assessment, bullying, psychophysiology, and research design.

# Chapter 1
# Introduction

**Abstract** This chapter provides an overview of sex trafficking including relevant terms and definitions, a discussion of the scope of the problem, and an exploration of commonly held myths and misconceptions. Additionally, this chapter describes the process of sex trafficking (i.e., acquisition, exploitation, exiting, and post-trafficking) and includes a discussion of those involved (i.e., sex traffickers, victims, sex buyers). This chapter will serve as a general framework for the topics covered in Chaps. 2, 3, 4, 5, and 6.

**Keywords** Sex trafficking · Victim · Sex trafficker · Sex buyer · Exploitation

## 1.1 Introduction

Sex trafficking constitutes a pervasive, global crime that violates the basic rights and humanity of men, women, and children. Traffickers are enticed by profit and the International Labour Organization (ILO) estimated that in 2014 $99 billion was generated from commercial sexual exploitation, reducing the human victims to no more than an objectified commodity. While traffickers profit, victims of sex trafficking endure significant and prolonged trauma resulting in a host of maladaptive physical, psychological, relational, and behavioral outcomes. In order to provide effective assistance to survivors, an awareness of the prevalence and process of sex trafficking is warranted as well as an understanding of the commonly held misconceptions and myths.

## 1.2 Terms

*Sex trafficking* is defined by the United States Congress in the Trafficking Victims Protection Act (TVPA, 2000) as "the recruitment, harboring, transportation, provision, or obtaining of a person for the purpose of a commercial sex act." Additionally,

 
J. Davidtz et al., *Sex Trafficking*, SpringerBriefs in Psychology,
https://doi.org/10.1007/978-3-031-09120-9_1

the TVPA stipulates *severe forms of trafficking in persons* to mean "sex trafficking in which a commercial sex act is induced by force, fraud, or coercion, or in which the person induced to perform such act has not attained 18 years of age."

*Coercion* is defined as:

> (a) threats of serious harm to or physical restraint against any person; (b) any scheme, plan, or pattern intended to cause a person to believe that failure to perform an act would result in serious harm to or physical restrain against any person; or (c) the abuse or threatened abuse of the legal process (TVPA, 2000).

The TVPA does not necessitate the presence of force, fraud, or coercion in the case of a minor indicating that a minor is legally unable to consent to a *commercial sex act*, defined in the TVPA (2000) as "any sex act on account of which anything of value is given to or received by any person."

Specifically pertaining to youth, *Commercial Sexual Exploitation of Children (CSEC)* was initially defined by the First World Congress against Commercial Sexual Exploitation of Children (1996) as "sexual abuse by an adult and remuneration in cash or kind to the child or a third person or persons." Specifically, CSEC occurs when the sexual abuse and exploitation of a child are exchanged for something of value or financially benefit an individual (Goldberg & Moore, 2018; Office of Juvenile Justice and Delinquency Prevention, 2014). Specific forms of CSEC include child sex trafficking or prostitution, child pornography, and sex tourism (i.e., traveling specifically for the purpose of sex), and these forms of CSEC frequently co-occur (Bissias et al., 2016; Centers for Disease Control [CDC], 2019; George & Panko, 2011; Miller-Perrin & Wurtele, 2017; OJJDP, 2014; Owens et al., 2016).

CSEC may also include *survival sex*, a term indicative of circumstances in which a minor may exchange sexual activities to obtain food, shelter, clothing, protection, or desired items such as drugs, either of their own volition or at the direction of another person (Goldberg & Moore, 2018; McNeal & Walker, 2016; Miller-Perrin & Wurtele, 2017; OJJDP, 2014). Other terms used interchangeably for survival sex include *self-trafficking*, *transactional sex*, and *sex trading* (Gerassi, 2015; Perkins & Ruiz, 2017). Various terms have been utilized within the literature to discuss child sex trafficking specifically including *juvenile sex trafficking (JST)*, *juvenile or child prostitution*, *sex trafficking of minors (STM)*, and *domestic minor sex trafficking (DMST)* (Gerassi, 2015; Goldberg & Moore, 2018; Hardy et al., 2013). The term DMST pertains specifically to minors born and trafficked within the United States (Goldberg & Moore, 2018; Sprang & Cole, 2018).

Sex trafficking may be conflated with *prostitution* or *sex work*; however, these terms are distinguished by conceptualizing prostitution as a voluntary, consensual sex act in the absence of force, fraud, or coercion (Gerassi, 2015; Schauer & Wheaton, 2006; Wilson & Butler, 2014). This distinction is noted in the U.S. Department of State (2020), which states that "prostitution by *willing adults* is not human trafficking regardless of whether it is legalized, decriminalized, or criminalized." Additionally, any individual under the age of 18 is legally unable to consent to prostitution, despite the potential presence of consent (Wilson & Butler, 2014).

Establishment of definitions in the TVPA (2000) and by the United Nations (UN, 2000) has assisted in uniformly defining sex trafficking and related terms. However, researchers continue to utilize an array of terms which overlap, conflict, and/or vary in meaning, thereby reducing clarity and conceptualization and thus leading to difficulties identifying and assisting victims (Countryman-Roswurm & Bolin, 2014; Ottisova et al., 2016; Rafferty, 2016). Consensus and consistency related to use of terms is imperative to improve the quality of research and understanding of sex trafficking (Okech et al., 2018; Ottisova et al., 2016).

## 1.3 Scope

Accurate estimations of this global issue have been exceedingly difficult to obtain. Despite these difficulties, varying rates from multiple sources illuminate the potential reach of sex trafficking. As stated in the Global Report on Trafficking in Persons, most victims of human trafficking are females, specifically adult women (approximately 42%), who are trafficked for the purpose of sexual exploitation (UNODC, 2021a). In 2019, per data from the United States National Human Trafficking Hotline, 14,597 victims of sex trafficking were identified, and 1,607 incidents of commercial sex acts were listed in the Uniform Crime Report (UCR, 2019). According to the ILO (2017), 4.8 million people were victims of forced sexual exploitation in 2016 in which women and girls accounted for more than 99% of all victims and 21% were children under the age of 18. Collecting accurate statistics has proven difficult due to an array of limitations: (a) the covert nature of the crime; (b) the absence of a uniform system of identification; (c) conflating, inconsistent, or conflicting definitions; (d) use of unclear or insufficient methodologies; (e) underreporting; (f) lack of resources; and (g) potential biases (Gerassi, 2015; Hardy et al., 2013; Rafferty, 2016; Schauer & Wheaton, 2006). Despite these challenges and the limited understanding of the true reach, sex trafficking remains an extensive and pervasive concern.

## 1.4 Common Myths

Commonly held myths and misconceptions regarding sex trafficking serve to perpetuate victim blame and to hinder efforts to mitigate sex trafficking and to identify victims (Franklin & Menaker, 2015; Haney et al., 2020; Rajaram & Tidball, 2018; Wiener et al., 2021). The most common myths and misconceptions regarding sex trafficking are described in Table 1.1.

**Table 1.1** The most common myths and misconceptions regarding sex trafficking

| Myth | Fact |
|---|---|
| Sex trafficking only occurs internationally. | Sex trafficking exists at a country, regional, and even state level (Department of Homeland Security [U.S. Department of Homeland Security], n.d.); Rajaram & Tidball, 2018.). In fact, a victim need not be transported at all to be considered a victim of sex trafficking under the TVPA (2000). |
| One may not be considered a victim of trafficking without the use of physical force or abuse. | Victims of trafficking may not experience physical force or abuse but may experience psychological abuse and coercion. Additionally, the presence of force, fraud, or coercion is not required when the individual is under the age of 18 (U.S. Department of Homeland Security, n.d.). |
| Only immigrants and foreign nationals are victims of sex trafficking. | According to the UNODC (2021a), most victims are trafficked "within geographically close areas" and are rescued within their country of origin. |
| Only women and girls are trafficked for sex. | Men and boys are additionally vulnerable to sex traffickers (Rajaram & Tidball, 2018). For example, Mlyakado and Li (2019) found rates of 26.2% and 14.8% for sexually exploited females and males in Tanzania, respectively. |
| All sex trafficking is facilitated by large, organized crime syndicates. | Traffickers may also work individually or in small groups. |
| Once victims are trafficked for sex they will seek help if they are around people or in public. | This is often not the case. Victims may be deterred by fear as traffickers often threaten to bring harm to both the victim and their loved ones should they attempt to seek help. Additionally, victim's identification documents are often confiscated which reduces their ability to seek assistance (U.S. Department of Homeland Security, n.d.). |
| There is a "stereotypical" victim of sex trafficking. | While certain factors may increase an individual's vulnerability, a victim of sex trafficking may be of any gender, ethnicity, age, race, nationality, and socioeconomic class (U.S. Department of Homeland Security, n.d.). |

## 1.5 Victims

Despite stereotypical media portrayals there exists no one common "narrative" for a victim of sex trafficking. Victims of sex trafficking are found both globally and domestically. They have been identified in all regions including cities, suburbs, and rural communities. Both impoverished regions and regions of high socioeconomic status are vulnerable to sex trafficking. Victims also vary in their level of education, citizenship, socioeconomic status, and migratory status. Despite the diversity apparent in the victimology of sex trafficking, factors that pose as risks for vulnerability have been identified and are discussed further.

### 1.5.1 Risk for Vulnerability

Risk factors for sex trafficking may best be viewed from an ecological perspective since an individual's level of vulnerability is the product of interactions among individual, familial, social, political, and economic factors (Goldberg & Moore, 2018; Miller-Perrin & Wurtele, 2017; Sanchez & Pacquiao, 2018). Individual risk factors comprise of age, gender, substance use, limited education, homelessness, high-risk sexual behaviors, migratory status, financial instability, unemployment, mental health conditions, and a previous history of victimization and abuse (Baidawi et al., 2020; Melgar et al., 2021; Naramore et al., 2017). Societal-level variables include a culture of tolerance, sexist ideologies, gender discrimination, poverty, high crime rates, police and government corruption, discrimination, and governmental policies (Buller et al., 2020; Gerassi, 2015; Sanchez & Pacquiao, 2018; Twis et al., 2020).

Risk for children and adolescents specifically is marked by a wide array of factors including childhood maltreatment; homelessness; runaway youth; throwaway youth (i.e., youth ejected from their home by their guardian); sexual and gender minorities; lack or absence of parental supervision; family dysfunction; criminal history; school failures; witnessing family violence; a history of physical, emotional, or sexual abuse; foster care and system-involved youth; and a history of mental or physical illness (Baidawi et al., 2020; Baird et al., 2020; Goldberg & Moore, 2018; Greeson et al., 2019; Hampton & Lieggi, 2020). Additionally, vulnerabilities specific to international youth have been cited to include unaccompanied immigrant minors, early separation from parents, forced marriage, being responsible for financially supporting their family, and pregnancy (Boyce et al., 2018; Hounmenou, 2016; Ijadi-Maghsoodi et al., 2016; Tsai, 2017). Studies have also identified intellectually and physically disabled youth as particularly vulnerable (Franchino-Olsen et al., 2020; Reid, 2016; Reid, 2018).

Certain risk factors appear to serve as pathways to other risks leading to an increased vulnerability for sex trafficking. Familial dysfunction, parental substance use, and childhood maltreatment, including abuse and neglect, have been found to lead to increased instances of homelessness, running away, and system placement in both juvenile detention centers and the child welfare system. This was seen in a study by Pullmann et al. (2020) who examined a sample of commercially sexually exploited children placed in the child welfare system. The authors found that 83% of youth had run away at least once while in system care and 40% were arrested and detained within the juvenile justice system due to "running away from state care." Thus, the pathways to vulnerabilities are complex and more research is needed to examine the nuanced interactions between vulnerabilities.

Youth are particularly vulnerable due to their age as well as associated behavioral and developmental needs (UNODC, 2021a; Sanchez & Pacquiao, 2018). Among children, consumers of sex trafficking have increasingly demanded victims of a younger age, and girls between the ages of 14 and 17 appear to be targeted at the highest rates; however, victimization is not exclusive to females (UNODC, 2021a; Wilson & Butler, 2014). In 2018, the National Center for Missing &

Exploited Children (NCMEC) analyzed 565 incidents of missing male children who were considered "endangered runaways" and "likely victims of child sex trafficking." Findings indicated that 21% of these incidents pertained to transgender females (i.e., identified as females and assigned male at birth). Little research has specifically examined vulnerabilities and experiences of male and sexual minority victims despite their presence both domestically and internationally (Moynihan et al., 2018). However, Shilo et al. (2021) examined a sample of commercially sexually exploited youth in Israel and found more similarities than differences in vulnerabilities between cisgender females, males, and transgender females. This was consistent with findings from Edinburgh et al. (2015) who interviewed professionals working with sex-trafficked minors. Results suggested no statistically significant differences in vulnerability factors, trafficking control and recruitment tactics, nor perceptions of victim needs (Cole, 2018). Some researchers have found male youth as more likely to participate in survival sex than female youth (Adjei & Saewyc, 2017; Cole, 2018). However, no research was found specifically pertaining to sexual minority youth victims or male-only samples.

#### 1.5.1.1 COVID-19

Considerations have also been given to the effects of the COVID-19 pandemic on the perpetuation of currently identified risk factors. Rates of homelessness and economic instability have been exacerbated by the global pandemic due to the economic impact and increasing rates of unemployment (UNODC, 2021b). Additionally, increased rates of child maltreatment resulting in hospitalization and intimate partner violence during the COVID-19 pandemic indicate a negative influence on the risk of vulnerability for sex trafficking. Moreover, the pandemic has resulted in elevated online time and activity, increasing risk of exposure to online predatory sex traffickers (UNODC, 2021b). Children may be particularly susceptible, especially in countries in which COVID-19 effects have resulted in the displacement and homelessness of youth (UNODC, 2021b). These amplified vulnerabilities leave victims more susceptible to sex traffickers who target individuals in need of economic assistance, shelter, and safety.

## 1.6 Sex Traffickers

Sex traffickers are enticed by profit in combination with their perceived low risk for detection and prosecution (Hardy et al., 2013; Hodge & Lietz, 2007; Polaris., 2018). There is no particular "profile" of a sex trafficker, as they have been found to vary in age, ethnicity, nationality, gender, and by specific offense (Tsagaris et al., 2017). Unfortunately, little distinct research has been conducted on sex traffickers due to challenges accessing this population. Some researchers have attempted to identify sex trafficker demographics, including Roe-Sepowitz (2019) who analyzed 1,416 sex traffickers of minors. Findings revealed that most of the sample were males (75.4%) ranging from 15 to 70 years old and were predominantly African American (71.7%). In support, Carpinteri et al. (2018) conducted a study of 98 known offenders of CSEC and found that being African American and unemployed were statistically significant predictors of engaging in sex trafficking. Additionally, Hargreaves-Cormany et al. (2016) found from a sample of 117 offenders of child sex trafficking that 95.7% were males and 91.5% were African American. In opposition; however, Tsagaris et al. (2017) examined offenders specifically of CSEC and found the sample to be predominately Caucasian males. These findings provide preliminary support for the development of more distinct profiles with increased research and suggests that varying profiles may be found for different types of offenses.

Some victims are recruited and exploited by the same trafficker(s), while others are recruited by one trafficker, exploited by another, and possibly transferred between the two by yet another trafficker termed *broker* (Shared Hope International, n.d.; UNODC, 2021a). A broker "facilitates the buying and selling of victims" (UNODC, 2021a). Sex traffickers may work alone, in collaboration with others, or within a more extensive criminal network and may be strangers, acquaintances, gangs, friends, intimate partners, or even family members (Baidawi et al., 2020; Goldberg & Moore, 2018; Reed et al., 2019; Roe-Sepowitz, 2019).

Most sex traffickers are adults; however, in 2021, 2% of the total federal trafficker convictions included boys and girls under the age of 18 (UNODC, 2021a). Youth as traffickers tend to learn from the modeled behaviors of older traffickers which are then emulated (Miccio-Fonseca, 2017b). There is unfortunately an extreme dearth of research available on youth as traffickers (Miccio-Fonseca, 2017a, b). Youth offenders may be recruited by family members, termed familial sex trafficking or family-facilitated sex trafficking, or may be recruited by the trafficker for the purposes of befriending and recruiting other minors (Goldberg & Moore, 2018; Miccio-Fonseca, 2017a, b). Miccio-Fonseca (2017b) created a potential profile of the juvenile sex trafficker based on compiled empirical data including victim reports. The profile depicted sex trafficking youth as excessively violent and sexually predatory, who demonstrate social proficiency and likely have a history of substance use, although no other research has been conducted to substantiate this proposed profile.

Based on governmental reports and the few studies that exist related to sex traffickers, the majority are male; however, there have been increasing numbers of identified female sex traffickers. Extant research has found female sex traffickers to be more involved in roles such as facilitation, transportation, and recruitment due to their enhanced accessibility to other victims and perceived trustworthiness (Broad, 2015; Miccio-Fonseca, 2017b; UNODC, 2021a). Additionally, female sex traffickers more often co-offend with a male counterpart and may be in an intimate relationship with the male trafficker (Broad, 2015; Carpinteri et al., 2018; Roe-Sepowitz et al., 2015). Roe-Sepowitz et al. (2015) identified five distinct typologies of female sex traffickers including: (a) madam/business partner, (b) family, (c) girilla, (d) handler, and (e) bottom defined in Table 1.2.

**Table 1.2** Typology of female sex trafficker

| Typology of female sex trafficker | Definition |
|---|---|
| Madam/business partner | Madams work as a manager and interact with victims like a business relationship. Madams frequently work alongside a male sex trafficker and provide managerial services (e.g., answering calls from sex buyers, setting up appointments with sex buyers, negotiating cost and location, transporting victims to appointments). |
| Family | Family-type female sex offenders act as caring and nurturing adults who provide safety and teaching to victims regarding the "the life" (i.e., involvement in sex trafficking). |
| Girilla | Girilla-type offenders utilize physical violence and force toward victims (as termed "gorilla pimp" for male sex traffickers) and are more frequently involved in international sex trafficking. |
| Handler | Handlers participate in the recruitment, harboring, and transportation of victims and are indirectly involved in sex trafficking. |
| Bottom | Bottoms are both offenders and victims working under a male sex trafficker. |

The sex traffickers' gender also appears to vary by region. For example, 80% of sex trafficker convictions in Central Asia and Eastern Europe were females (UNODC, 2021a).

Sex trafficking can be facilitated by large or small scale organized crime syndicates who participate in an array of criminal activities such as drug and arms trafficking (Lebov, 2010; Viuhko, 2010). Two distinguishable types of organized criminal groups have been identified: *governance-type* and *business enterprise-type* (UNODC, 2021a). The business enterprise-type consists of "three or more traffickers systematically working together to traffic persons as a core component of their criminal activities;" whereas the governance-type "practice security governance in a community or territory by means of fear and violence and may be involved in multiple illicit markets" (UNODC, 2021a). The relationship between organized crime and human trafficking has been contested, with some claiming little empirical support and others claiming the sex trafficking industry is dominated by organized criminal groups (Hodge, 2008). For example, Tripp and McMahon-Howard (2016) conducted one study using data from 24 federal human trafficking cases indicted in Atlanta between 2000 and 2013 and findings indicated little relationship with organized crime. However, more research is needed in this area to determine the true extent of the relationship of organized crime groups to human trafficking in general and sex trafficking specifically.

### 1.6.1 Bottom

The understanding the *bottom* is complex as their role is both as victim and as offender. A bottom is a role appointed to a victim by a sex trafficker in which the bottom maintains the highest status of all the victims (Broad, 2015; Goldberg & Moore, 2018; Roe-Sepowitz et al., 2015). This position is used as a control tactic to manipulate victims into competing for the perceived benefits of obtaining this role, thus increasing the victim's psychological dependence on their sex trafficker (Herrington & McEachern, 2018). Sex traffickers may allocate one individual as the bottom or may alternate among victims as a punishment or reward (Crocker, 2017). Frequently, the bottom role is appointed to the victim who has earned the most money, has been with the trafficker the longest, or is the most trusted (Roe-Sepowitz, 2019; Roe-Sepowitz et al., 2015). The offering of the role is often accompanied by false promises of benefits, such as reduced exposure to violence and the ability to keep a portion of their earnings. Further, the bottom may believe that they will be exposed to less sex work if they are able to recruit other victims. The bottom is also utilized by the trafficker to assist in offending behaviors such as recruiting victims, collecting victim's pay, training and transporting victims, supervising victims, posting advertisements, and allocating punishment (Goldberg & Moore, 2018; Roe-Sepowitz et al., 2015). Roe-Sepowitz et al. (2015) found bottoms to be involved with the largest sex trafficking rings compared to other female sex traffickers and were most likely to be African American. However, little research has been conducted on a consistent profile. Bottoms offend against other victims; however, they are also victims themselves and have suffered the same history of recruitment, coercion, and abuse (Broad, 2015; Roe-Sepowitz et al., 2015).

## 1.7 Sex Buyers

Sex buyers sustain the demand for sex trafficking and their prevalence is unknown. Furthermore, there is a dearth of information regarding these individuals and the majority of the research has focused specifically on consumers of child sexual exploitation materials (Babchishin et al., 2018; Christensen & Tsagaris, 2020). Despite the research limitations, there is a clear sexual motive of sex buyers. Demographically, research has found that sex buyers are majority male. In addition, Carpinteri et al. (2018) found employment status significantly predicted engagement as a producer or sex buyer such that the odds were 1.5 times greater for those unemployed. Additionally, the researchers found that being African American significantly predicted engaging as a producer or sex buyer with odds 11.62 times greater (Carpinteri et al., 2018). These findings provide a basis for future research to explore factors associated with the buyers of sex trafficking. The language of terms vary regarding persons who buy sexual acts from victims. Terms utilized include *john*, *client*, *consumer*, *customer*, *patron*, and *fautor* (Schauer & Wheaton,

2006). Sex buyers can be organized into three different categories including situational, preferential, and opportunistic (Jordan et al., 2013). A situational sex buyer typically purchases sex acts based on availability while opportunistic buyers purchase sex indiscriminately. Preferential buyers purchase sex acts based on a specific sexual preference such as a specific age or gender (Jordan et al., 2013).

## 1.8 Process

### *1.8.1 Acquisition*

Victims may be targeted in a variety of settings such as at school, foster care homes, bus stops, parties, churches, malls, online, and within their own residences (Baird et al., 2020; Beckett & Schubotz, 2014; Miccio-Fonseca, 2017b). Sex traffickers often facilitate a process, termed *grooming*, in which the trust of the victim is gained by establishing an initial relationship, such as a friendship or as an intimate partner. Subsequently, the sex trafficker provides a desired need such as love, attachment, material items, housing, food, drugs, or false promises (Baird et al., 2020; Goldberg & Moore, 2018; Hargreaves-Cormany & Patterson, 2016). Sex traffickers exploit preexisting individual vulnerabilities such as the innate desire for love, protection, or connection, financial instability, substance use, or family dysfunction and offer associated false promises of employment, love, monetary gain, marriage, housing, or safety and stability, prior to exploitation (Cecchet & Thoburn, 2014; Duncan & DeHart, 2019; Wilson & Butler, 2014). For example, sex traffickers may intentionally target impoverished families and extend false promises of income and improved livelihood, convincing the families to sell their children for profit (Hodge, 2008; Hodge & Lietz, 2007). Other victims may be deceived by false-front agencies (e.g., modeling, marriage) which may even be legitimate businesses (Hodge, 2008; Hodge & Lietz, 2007).

A myriad of other techniques utilized by sex traffickers include physical and sexual coercion, posing as an intimate partner (termed *Romeo Pimp*), and kidnapping or abduction (Duncan & DeHart, 2019; Miller-Perrin & Wurtele, 2017; Reid, 2016; UNODC, 2021a). Some sex traffickers may target individuals working within the sex industry as sex workers, who, while aware of the potential sex work, are unaware of the abusive conditions in which they will be forced to work (Hodge, 2008). Using statistics generated from data from the United States National Human Trafficking Hotline, researchers identified the top five recruitment tactics in 2019 as (a) intimate partner/marriage proposition, (b) familial recruiting, (c) job offers/advertisement, (d) posing as a benefactor, and (e) false promises/fraud. Internationally; however, cultural customs and traditions may result in victims being sold in to trafficking (Jani & Felke, 2017; Lau, 2008). Therefore, it is important to note that researchers have found the dominant recruitment tactics vary by location (Hodge, 2008).

#### 1.8.1.1 The Role of Technology

Technological advances have increased the ease and anonymity with which traffickers can operate and locate potential victims (O'Brien & Li, 2020). Social media is frequently utilized by sex traffickers to facilitate the grooming process by "befriending" a potential victim or initiating an intimate relationship (Baird et al., 2020; Goldberg & Moore, 2018; Sanchez & Pacquiao, 2018; Wells et al., 2012). Additionally, online avenues are often utilized by traffickers to facilitate the advertisement and purchase of victims, including the sale of sexually exploitative materials and online escort services (O'Brien & Li, 2020; Roe-Sepowitz, 2019). Sex traffickers frequent Internet sites where they can communicate and connect with sex buyers (Mitchell et al., 2011; O'Brien & Li, 2020; Roe-Sepowitz, 2019). Furthermore, sex traffickers utilize technology as a means to track and control their victims (O'Brien & Li, 2020).

### *1.8.2 Exploitation*

Following recruitment, some victims of sex trafficking may be transported via car, air, boat, or train, both internationally and intranationally, while others are not transported at all (Wilson & Butler, 2014). Victims often endure captivity and restriction of their movements, hindering feelings of autonomy and eliminating connections to others outside of the sex trade (Herrington & McEachern, 2018; Wilson & Butler, 2013). Victims may be held in unsanitary and crowded living conditions where they experience disruptions in sleep and malnutrition among other issues (Wilson & Butler, 2014). Additionally, victims are expected to work for little to no pay, for extensive hours, and in hazardous conditions with no say in the sex buyers who are serviced, the price of services, the use of protection (e.g., condoms, birth control), or the type of sexual services enacted (Goldberg et al., 2013; Hossain et al., 2010; Jordan et al., 2013; Meshkovska et al., 2015). Insight into the specific experiences of exploitation during sex trafficking is lacking; however, researchers have shown, in the case of familial specific sex trafficking, youth are often exploited by family members to perform sex acts in exchange for money or drugs (Kotrla, 2010; Miccio-Fonseca, 2017b). More research is needed to gain insight on the specific experiences of victims during exploitation.

#### 1.8.2.1 Maintaining Control

Traffickers execute control tactics in the form of physical, psychological, and sexual abuse of the victims. Victims may be beat, shot, stabbed, starved, burned, tortured, sexually assaulted, drugged, neglected, and deprived of basic needs and medical attention (Herrington & McEachern, 2018; Meshkovska et al., 2015; Miller-Perrin & Wurtele, 2017). Additionally, traffickers instill fear by simultaneously utilizing intimidation, deception, blackmail, and threats against the victim and their families and friends (Hampton & Lieggi, 2020; Jordan et al., 2013; Miller-Perrin & Wurtele, 2017). Traffickers also use substances to create control over victims with previous dependency problems or may initiate substance use with victims who had never previously used (Twis et al., 2020; U.S. Department of State, 2020; Wilson & Butler, 2014). Following the creation of a substance dependency, sex traffickers may threaten withdrawal if the victim refuses to comply in forced engagement in sexual acts (U.S. Department of State, 2020).

Victims may also be relocated to create confusion and unfamiliarity with their surroundings. Furthermore, sex traffickers may confiscate identifying documents (e.g., passports, birth certificates) to limit the victim's ability to seek help and to diminish their sense of identity (Jordan et al., 2013 Lebov, 2010; Viuhko, 2010). Victims' names may be changed or victims may be assigned a number to further dehumanize them into a commodity (Herrington & McEachern, 2018). Victims typically are not provided access to medical services or other necessary treatments due to the possibility that a victim may disclose their captivity (Barnert et al., 2019). Victims' movements are also frequently restricted, monitored, and regulated. Using the aforementioned tactics sex traffickers create a loss of identity, reduced individual autonomy, and foster high levels of dependence.

Financial control is also exerted as sex traffickers often keep any payment received from forced sexual services (Ijadi-Maghsoodi et al., 2016; Reid, 2016). *Debt bondage* occurs as a form of psychological coercion in which a bond or debt is imposed on the victim by the sex trafficker (Reid, 2016). Efforts to pay off the "debt" are made to be impossible due to added fees, interest, and inherited debt (Hodge, 2008; Viuhko, 2010). Additional fees may be allocated by the sex trafficker for "travel costs" or as a punishment for breaking rules created by the sex trafficker (e.g., if victims do not meet a specific quota of sexual exchanges) (Viuhko, 2010). This results in the victim being forced to engage in increased sex acts to pay off the unreachable amount, thus destroying hope and reducing the victim's capacity to escape (UNODC, 2021a; U.S. Department of State, 2020).

*Trauma bonding*, also known as "Stockholm syndrome," has been seen to occur between victims and their sex traffickers (Hardy et al., 2013; Hom & Woods, 2013; Ijadi-Maghsoodi et al., 2016; Miccio-Fonseca, 2017b). Trauma bonding is a phenomenon in which the victim comes to develop a strong emotional connection with their trafficker. This is due to the power imbalance between the trafficker and victim, in which the trafficker allocates both rewards and punishment intermittently during cycles of abuse, thereby creating confusion and dependence in the victim (Herrington & McEachern, 2018; U.S. Department of State, 2020). Sex traffickers may maintain a role of "protector" or "caretaker" to foster a sense of dependency, reliance, connection, and loyalty (Rafferty, 2016; Reid, 2016; U.S. Department of State, 2020). The victims' attachment toward the sex trafficker may already preexist in cases in which the sex trafficker is a parent, family member, or intimate partner. Trauma bonding thought to develop to enhance survival, as the victim becomes reliant upon the trafficker for emotional support and for their basic needs. This can create an attachment with the sex trafficker and a sense of gratitude for the sex trafficker while simultaneously fearing prospective abuse and punishment (Goldberg & Moore, 2018; Hardy et al., 2013; Herrington & McEachern, 2018). Sex traffickers purposefully isolate victims both individually and systematically to diminish external support systems. As a result, victims will look to their sex traffickers in an attempt to receive the desired care and support (Cecchet & Thoburn, 2014; Reid, 2016; U.S. Department of State, 2020). Not all victims experience trauma bonding; however, youth are particularly susceptible as well as individuals who lack access to housing, healthcare, employment, income, education, and asylum (Goldberg & Moore, 2018; Rafferty, 2016; U.S. Department of State, 2020).

### *1.8.3 Exiting*

The exiting process is unique to each victim and may be via escape or identification by law enforcement or other service agencies (e.g., child welfare system, emergency room department) (Duncan & DeHart, 2019). A complex interaction of variables contributes to the difficulties of exiting sex trafficking. Barriers include a lack of knowledge regarding resources and services; a distrust of law enforcement and other helping professionals; and having no external support system (Mumey et al., 2021; Wilson, 2019). Furthermore, threats of violence are often made by the sex trafficker(s) against the individual and their family and friends, creating immense fear that also reduces a victim's likelihood to attempt escape. The victim may experience ambivalence and conflicting emotions when considering exiting, particularly when trauma bonding has occurred with the sex trafficker(s) (Wilson & Butler, 2014; Wilson, 2019). They may feel dependent on the sex trafficker(s) for their basic needs including shelter, food, clothes, and finances (Mumey et al., 2021). Victims may also feel entrapped as they frequently lack the skills and education needed to obtain employment. Furthermore, victims may be unable to obtain employment if the sex trafficker has confiscated their identifying documents or if they have a criminal record (Wilson & Butler, 2014; Wilson, 2019). Many victims are forced by their sex traffickers to commit crimes or have been arrested for prostitution, thus initiating system involvement. Further, they may maintain negative self-beliefs including feelings of disgust, shame, and guilt which combine with experiences of societal stigma, discrimination, and negative attitudes regarding sexuality and gender, perpetuating isolation and feelings of ostracization (Cecchet & Thoburn, 2014; Hampton & Lieggi, 2020; Wilson & Butler, 2014; Wilson, 2019). The cumulation of the aforementioned barriers create an overwhelmingly complex process for the victim to navigate that greatly deters exiting.

#### 1.8.3.1 Identification

One means of potential exit is through identification. Identification occurs when an individual encounters various outside personnel and, as a result, is recognized as a victim of sex trafficking and is assisted in exiting the sex trafficking situation

(Ijadi-Maghsoodi et al., 2014). Victims may be identified by medical personnel, mental health professionals, law enforcement, and other service providers (Ijadi-Maghsoodi et al., 2014; Mumey et al., 2021). Unfortunately, victims often go unidentified due to fear of disclosure, particularly if their trafficker is present or has accompanied them to appointments (Barnert et al., 2019). Additionally, some victims may be afraid to disclose due to shame, stigma, or for fear of deportation. Others may not perceive themselves as victims or do not want to be identified (Rafferty, 2016). Additionally, community members and health professionals may not be aware of the indicators that someone may be a victim of sex trafficking, resulting in a missed opportunity to identify the victim and assist their escape (Albright et al., 2020; Goldberg & Moore, 2018).

### *1.8.4 Post-trafficking*

Reintegration and recovery post-trafficking presents extensive difficulties for the survivor, frequently resulting in re-trafficking (Goldberg & Moore, 2018). Victims often experience multiple cycles of exit and reentry prior to completing a successful exit from sex trafficking due to the aforementioned barriers (Goldberg & Moore, 2018; Hampton & Lieggi, 2020; Helpingstine et al., 2021). The likelihood of successful exit increases when the victim can receive higher levels of support and increased access to resources and assistance.

## 1.9 Conclusion

Despite difficulties understanding the true scope, sex trafficking is acknowledged as a pervasive crime affecting victims both globally and domestically. Common myths and misconceptions hinder identification and assistance efforts for this pervasive crime as well as simultaneously impede survivors' ability to heal from trafficking experiences. While victims are frequently targeted for preexisting vulnerabilities, they are of all races, ages, genders, ethnicities, and nationalities. Some sex traffickers force individuals into sex trafficking while others manipulate and coerce victims with false promises of love, money, and employment. Sex trafficking victims endure harrowing living conditions and repeated physical, emotional, sexual, and psychological abuse. Exploitation includes extensive hours servicing clients of the trafficker's choosing, with no say in sex acts performed nor amount of money earned. These individuals are dehumanized, exploited, and objectified until they are either identified by external personnel or able to escape. These endured experiences are detrimental to the survivors' physical and mental health. Thus, a comprehensive understanding of the process of sex trafficking is an important first step in the successful identification and treatment of victims and survivors.

## References


Adjei, J. K., & Saewyc, E. M. (2017, March). Boys are not exempt: Sexual exploitation of adolescents in sub-Saharan Africa. *Child Abuse & Neglect, 65*, 14–23.

Albright, K., Greenbaum, J., Edwards, S. A., & Tsai, C. (2020, February). Systematic review of facilitators of, barriers to, and recommendations for healthcare services for child survivors of human trafficking globally. *Child Abuse & Neglect, 100*.

Babchishin, K. M., Merdian, H. L., Bartels, R. M., & Perkins, D. (2018). Child sexual exploitation materials offenders: A review. *European Psychologist, 23*(2), 130–143.

Baidawi, S., Sheehan, R., & Flynn, C. (2020, November). Criminal exploitation of child protection-involved youth. *Children and Youth Services Review, 118*.

Baird, K., McDonald, K. P., & Connolly, J. (2020, January). Sex trafficking of women and girls in a southern Ontario region: Police file review exploring victim characteristics, trafficking experiences, and the intersection with child welfare. *Canadian Journal of Behavioural Science, 52*(1), 8–17.

Barnert, E., Kelly, M., Godoy, S., Abrams, L. S., Rasch, M., et al. (2019). Understanding commercially sexually exploited young women's access to, utilization of, and engagement in health care: "Work around what I need". *Women's Health Issues, 29*(4), 315–324.

Beckett, H., & Schubotz, D. (2014, April). Young people's self-reported experiences of sexual exploitation and sexual violence: A view from Northern Ireland. *Journal of Youth Studies, 17*(4), 430–445.

Bissias, G., Levine, B., Liberatore, M., Lynn, B., More, J., et al. (2016, February). Characterization of contact offenders and child exploitation material trafficking on five peer-to-peer networks. *Child Abuse & Neglect, 52*, 185–199.

Boyce, S. C., Brouwer, K. C., Triplett, D., Servin, A. E., Magis-Rodriguez, C., et al. (2018, August). Childhood experiences of sexual violence, pregnancy, and marriage associated with child sex trafficking among female sex workers in two U.S.-Mexico border cities. *American Journal of Public Health, 108*(8), 1049–1054.

Broad, R. (2015, November). 'A vile and violent thing': Female traffickers and the criminal justice response. *British Journal of Criminology, 55*(6), 1058–1075.

Buller, A. M., Pichon, M., McAlpine, A., Cislaghi, B., Heise, L., et al. (2020, June). Systematic review of social norms, attitudes, and factual beliefs linked to the sexual exploitation of children and adolescents. *Child Abuse & Neglect, 104*.

Carpinteri, A., Bang, B., Klimley, K., Black, R. A., & Van Hasselt, V. B. (2018, June). Commercial sexual exploitation of children: An assessment of offender characteristics. *Journal of Police and Criminal Psychology, 33*(2), 150–157.

Cecchet, S. J., & Thoburn, J. (2014, September). The psychological experience of child and adolescent sex trafficking in the United States: Trauma and resilience in survivors. *Psychological Trauma: Theory, Research, Practice, and Policy, 6*(5), 482–493.

Centers for Disease Control and Prevention. (2019, November 18). *Sex tourism.* U.S. Department of Health and Human Services. https://wwwnc.cdc.gov/travel/page/sex-tourism

Christensen, L. S., & Tsagaris, G. S. (2020, April). *Offenders convicted of child sexual exploitation material offences: Characteristics of offenders and an exploration of judicial censure.* Psychiatry, Psychology and Law.

Cole, J. (2018, August). Service providers' perspectives on sex trafficking of male minors: Comparing background and trafficking situations of male and female victims. *Child & Adolescent Social Work Journal, 35*(4), 423–433.

Countryman-Roswurm, K., & Bolin, B. L. (2014). Domestic minor sex trafficking: Assessing and reducing risk. *Child and Adolescent Social Work Journal, 31*(6), 521–538.

Crocker, S. (2017). Stripping agency from top to bottom: The need for a sentencing guideline safety valve for bottoms prosecuted under the federal sex trafficking statutes. *Northwestern University Law Review, 111*(3), 753–791.

Duncan, A. C., & DeHart, D. (2019, May). Provider perspectives on sex trafficking: Victim pathways, service needs, & blurred boundaries. *Victims & Offenders, 14*(4), 510–531.

Edinburgh, L., Pape-Blabolil, J., Harpin, S. B., & Saewyc, E. (2015, August). Assessing exploitation experiences of girls and boys seen at a Child Advocacy Center. *Child Abuse & Neglect, 46*, 47–59.

First World Congress against Commercial Sexual Exploitation of Children. (1996). *Declaration and Agenda for Action*. Available at: http://www.csecworldcongress.org/PDF/en/Stockholm/Outcome_documents/Stockholm%20Declaration%201996_EN.pdf

Franchino-Olsen, H., Silverstein, H. A., Kahn, N. F., & Martin, S. L. (2020). Minor sex trafficking of girls with disabilities. *International Journal of Human Rights in Healthcare, 13*(2), 97–108.

Franklin, C. A., & Menaker, T. A. (2015, April). The impact of observer characteristics on blame assessments of prostituted female youth. *Feminist Criminology, 10*(2), 140–164.

George, B. P., & Panko, T. R. (2011, June). Child sex tourism: Facilitating conditions, legal remedies, and other interventions. *Vulnerable Children and Youth Studies, 6*(2), 134–143.

Gerassi, L. (2015, August). From exploitation to industry: Definitions, risks, and consequences of domestic sexual exploitation and sex work among women and girls. *Journal of Human Behavior in the Social Environment, 25*(6), 591–605.

Goldberg, A., & Moore, J. (2018, January). Domestic minor sex trafficking. *Child and Adolescent Psychiatric Clinics of North America, 27*(1), 77–92.

Goldberg, S. M., Rangel, G., Staines, H., Vera, A., Lozada, R., et al. (2013, Aug). Individual, interpersonal, and social-structural correlates of involuntary sex exchange among female sex workers in two Mexico-U.S. border cities. *Journal of Acquired Immune Deficiency Syndromes, 63*(5), 639–646.

Greeson, J. K. P., Treglia, D., Wolfe, D. S., & Wasch, S. (2019, June). Prevalence and correlates of sex trafficking among homeless and runaway youths presenting for shelter services. *Social Work Research, 43*(2), 91–99.

Hampton, M. D., & Lieggi, M. (2020, January). Commercial sexual exploitation of youth in the United States: A qualitative systematic review. *Trauma, Violence, & Abuse, 21*(1), 57–70.

Haney, K., LeBeau, K., Bodner, S., Czizik, A., Young, M. E., et al. (2020). Sex trafficking in the United States: A scoping review. *Journal of Evidence-Based Social Work, 17*(6), 714–748.

Hardy, V. L., Compton, K. D., & McPhatter, V. S. (2013, February). Domestic minor sex trafficking: Practice implications for mental health professionals. *Journal of Women & Social Work, 28*(1), 8–18.

Hargreaves-Cormany, H. A., & Patterson, T. D. (2016). Characteristics of survivors of juvenile sex trafficking: Implications for treatment and intervention initiatives. *Aggression and Violent Behavior, 30*, 32–39.

Hargreaves-Cormany, H. A., Patterson, T. D., Muirhead, Y. E., Bureau, F., & of Investigation. (2016). A typology of offenders engaging in the sex trafficking of juveniles (STJ): Implications for risk assessment. *Aggression and Violent Behavior, 30*, 40–47.

Helpingstine, C. E., Stephens, D. P., Kenny, M. C., & Eaton, A. A. (2021, May). Adolescent girls with a history of Commercial Sexual Exploitation (CSE): Perceptions and characteristics of social networks. *Child Abuse & Neglect*, 115.

Herrington, R. L., & McEachern, P. (2018, July). "Breaking her spirit" through objectification, fragmentation, and consumption: A conceptual framework for understanding domestic sex trafficking. *Journal of Aggression, Maltreatment & Trauma, 27*(6), 598–611.

Hodge, D. R. (2008, April). Sexual trafficking in the United States: A domestic problem with transnational dimensions. *Social Work, 53*(2), 143–152.

Hodge, D. R., & Lietz, C. A. (2007). The international sexual trafficking of women and children: A review of the literature. *Journal of Women & Social Work, 22*(2), 163–174.

Hom, K. A., & Woods, S. J. (2013, Feb). Trauma and its aftermath for commercially sexually exploited women as told by front-line service providers. *Issues in Mental Health Nursing, 34*(2), 75–81.

Hossain, M., Zimmerman, C., Abas, M., Light, M., & Watts, C. (2010, December). The relationship of trauma to mental disorder among trafficked and sexually exploited girls and women. *American Journal of Public Health, 100*(12), 2442–2449.

Hounmenou, C. (2016, September). Exploring child prostitution in a major city in the west African region. *Child Abuse & Neglect, 59*, 26–35.

Ijadi-Maghsoodi, R., Todd, E. J., & Bath, E. P. J. (2014, August). Commercial sexual exploitation of children and the role of the child psychiatrist. *Journal of the American Academy of Child & Adolescent Psychiatry, 53*(8), 825–829.

Ijadi-Maghsoodi, R., Cook, M., Barnert, E. S., Gaboian, S., & Bath, E. (2016, January). Understanding and responding to the needs of commercially sexually exploited youth: Recommendations for the mental health provider. *Child and Adolescent Psychiatric Clinics of North America, 25*(1), 107–122.

International Labour Office, Walk Free Foundation, & International Organization for Migration. (2017). *Global estimates of modern slavery.* https://www.ilo.org/wcmsp5/groups/public/%2D%2D-dgreports/%2D%2D-dcomm/documents/publication/wcms_575479.pdf

Jani, N., & Felke, T. P. (2017, July). Gender bias and sex-trafficking in Indian society. *International Social Work, 60*(4), 831–846.

Jordan, J., Patel, B., & Rapp, L. (2013). Domestic minor sex trafficking: A social work perspective on misidentification, victims, buyers, traffickers, treatment, and reform of current practice. *Journal of Human Behavior in the Social Environment, 23*(3), 356–369.

Kotrla, K. (2010). Domestic minor sex trafficking in the United States. *Social Work, 55*(2), 181–187.

Lau, C. (2008, January). Child prostitution in Thailand. *Journal of Child Health Care, 12*(2), 44–155.

Lebov, K. (2010). Human trafficking in Scotland. *European Journal of Criminology, 7*(1), 77–93.

McNeal, B. A., & Walker, J. T. (2016). Parental effects on the exchange of sex for drugs or money in adolescents. *American Journal of Criminal Justice, 41*(4), 710–731.

Melgar, P., Merodio, G., Duque, E., & Ramis-Salas, M. (2021, January). "Petites Bonnes" minors sex trafficked in Morocco and Spain. *Children and Youth Services Review, 120.*

Meshkovska, B., Siegel, M., Stutterheim, S. E., & Bos, A. E. (2015). Female sex trafficking: Conceptual issues, current debates, and future directions. *Journal of Sex Research, 52*(4), 380–395.

Miccio-Fonseca, L. C. (2017a). Juvenile female sex traffickers. *Aggression and Violent Behavior, 35*, 26–32.

Miccio-Fonseca, L. C. (2017b, May). The anomaly among sexually abusive youth: The juvenile sex trafficker. *Journal of Aggression, Maltreatment, & Trauma, 26*(5), 558–572.

Miller-Perrin, C., & Wurtele, S. K. (2017). Sex trafficking and the commercial sexual exploitation of children. *Women & Therapy, 40*(1–2), 123–151.

Mitchell, K. J., Jones, L. M., Finkelhor, D., & Wolak, J. (2011, March). Internet-facilitated commercial sexual exploitation of children: Findings from a nationally representative sample of law enforcement agencies in the United States. *Sexual Abuse: Journal of Research and Treatment, 23*(1), 43–71.

Mlyakado, B. P., & Li, J. C.-M. (2019, May). Sexual exploitation of adolescent students in Tanzania: Implications for social services. *International Social Work, 62*(3), 1104–1116.

Moynihan, M., Mitchell, K., Pitcher, C., Havaei, F., Ferguson, M., et al. (2018, February). A systematic review of the state of the literature on sexually exploited boys internationally. *Child Abuse & Neglect, 76*, 440–451.

Mumey, A., Sardana, S., Richardson-Vejlgaard, R., & Akinsulure-Smith, A. M. (2021, February). Mental health needs of sex trafficking survivors in New York City: Reflections on exploitation, coping, and recovery. *Psychological Trauma: Theory, Research, Practice, and Policy, 13*(2), 185–192.

Naramore, R., Bright, M. A., Epps, N., & Hardt, N. S. (2017, June). Youth arrested for trading sex have the highest rates of childhood adversity: A statewide study of juvenile offenders. *Sexual Abuse: Journal of Research and Treatment, 29*(4), 396–410.

O'Brien, J. E., & Li, W. (2020, May). The role of the internet in the grooming, exploitation, and exit of the United States domestic minor sex trafficking victims. *Journal of Children and Media, 14*(2), 187–203.

Office of Juvenile Justice and Delinquency Prevention. (2014). *Commercial sexual exploitation of children. U.S. Department of Justice*. https://ojjdp.ojp.gov/programs/commercial-sexual-exploitation-children

Okech, D., Choi, Y. J., Elkins, J., & Burns, A. C. (2018). Seventeen years of human trafficking research in social work: A review of the literature. *Journal of Evidence-Informed Social Work, 15*(2), 103–122.

Ottisova, L., Hemmings, S., Howard, L. M., Zimmerman, C., & Oram, S. (2016, August). Prevalence and risk of violence and the mental, physical and sexual health problems associated with human trafficking: An updated systematic review. *Epidemiology and Psychiatric Sciences, 25*(4), 317–341.

Owens, J. N., Eakin, J. D., Hoffer, T., Muirhead, Y., & Shelton, J. L. E. (2016). Investigative aspects of crossover offending from a sample of FBI online child sexual exploitation cases. *Aggression and Violent Behavior, 30*, 3–14.

Perkins, E. B., & Ruiz, C. (2017, April). Domestic minor sex trafficking in a rural state: Interviews with adjudicated female juveniles. *Child & Adolescent Social Work Journal, 34*(2), 171–180.

Polaris. (2018, July) *On-ramps, intersections, and exit routes: A roadmap for systems and industries to prevent and disrupt human trafficking*. https://polarisproject.org/wp-content/uploads/2018/08/A-Roadmap-for-Systems-and-Industries-to-Prevent-and-Disrupt-Human-Trafficking-Health-Care.pdf

Pullmann, M. D., Roberts, N., Parker, E. M., Mangiaracina, K. J., Briner, L., et al. (2020, April). Residential instability, running away, and juvenile detention characterizes commercially sexually exploited youth involved in Washington state's child welfare system. *Child Abuse & Neglect, 102*.

Rafferty, Y. (2016, February). Challenges to the rapid identification of children who have been trafficked for commercial sexual exploitation. *Child Abuse & Neglect, 52*, 158–168.

Rajaram, S. S., & Tidball, S. (2018). Survivors' voices – Complex needs of sex trafficking survivors in the Midwest. *Behavioral Medicine, 44*(3), 189–198.

Reed, S. M., Kennedy, M. A., Decker, M. R., & Cimino, A. N. (2019, April). Friends, family, and boyfriends: An analysis of relationship pathways into commercial sexual exploitation. *Child Abuse & Neglect, 90*, 1–12.

Reid, J. A. (2016, September). Entrapment and enmeshment schemes used by sex traffickers. *Sexual Abuse: Journal of Research and Treatment, 28*(6), 491–511.

Reid, J. A. (2018, March). Sex trafficking of girls with intellectual disabilities: An exploratory mixed methods study. *Sexual Abuse: Journal of Research and Treatment, 30*(2), 107–131.

Roe-Sepowitz, D. (2019, July). A six-year analysis of sex traffickers of minors: Exploring characteristics and sex trafficking patterns. *Journal of Human Behavior in the Social Environment, 29*(5), 608–629.

Roe-Sepowitz, D. E., Gallagher, J., Risinger, M., & Hickle, K. (2015, October). The sexual exploitation of girls in the United States: The role of female pimps. *Journal of Interpersonal Violence, 30*(16), 2814–2830.

Sanchez, R. V., & Pacquiao, D. F. (2018). An ecological approach toward prevention and care of victims of domestic minor sex trafficking. *Journal of Forensic Nursing, 14*(2), 98–105.

Schauer, E. J., & Wheaton, E. M. (2006). Sex trafficking into the United States: A literature review. *Criminal Justice Review, 31*(2), 146–169.

Shared Hope International. (n.d.). *Trafficking terms*. https://sharedhope.org/the-problem/trafficking-terms/

Shilo, G., Preis, H., & Peled, E. (2021). Gender differences among commercially sexually exploited youth in Israel. *Child Abuse Review, 30*(1), 32–47.

Sprang, G., & Cole, J. (2018). Familial sex trafficking of minors: Trafficking conditions, clinical presentation, and system involvement. *Journal of Family Violence, 33*(3), 185–195.

Trafficking Victims Protection Act of 2000, 22 U.S.C. (b) (2) § 7101 (2000).

Tripp, T. M., & McMahon-Howard, J. (2016). Perception vs. reality: The relationship between organized crime and human trafficking in metropolitan Atlanta. *American Journal of Criminal Justice, 41*, 732–764.

Tsagaris, G. S., Bach, J. E., & Cimino, C. (2017, May). The characteristics of federal offenders sentenced for sexual exploitation of children within a large urban metropolitan region. *Journal of Sexual Aggression, 23*(2), 181–194.

Tsai, L. C. (2017, May). Family financial roles assumed by sex trafficking survivors upon community re-entry: Findings from a financial diaries study in the Philippines. *Journal of Human Behavior in the Social Environment, 27*(4), 334–345.

Twis, M. K., Kirschner, L., & Greenwood, D. (2020, July). Trafficked by a friend: A qualitative analysis of adolescent trafficking victims' archival case files. *Child & Adolescent Social Work Journal.*

United Nations. (2000). *Protocol to prevent, suppress and punish trafficking in persons, especially women and children, supplementing the United Nations Convention Against Transnational Organized Crime.* Retrieved from https://treaties.un.org/doc/Publication/MTDSG/Volume%20II/Chapter%20XVIII/xviii-12-a.en.pdf

United Nations Office on Drugs and Crime. (2021a, January). *Global report on trafficking in persons 2020.* https://www.unodc.org/documents/dataandanalysis/tip/2021/GLOTiP_2020_15jan_web.pdf

United Nations Office on Drugs and Crime. (2021b, February). *COVID-19 seen worsening overall trend in human trafficking.* https://www.unodc.org/unodc/frontpage/2021/February/share-of-children-among-trafficking-victims-increases%2D%2Dboys-five-times-covid-19-seen-worsening-overall-trend-in-human-trafficking%2D%2Dsays-unodc-report.html

Uniform Crime Reporting Program. (2019). *2019 Crime in the United States.* Criminal Justice Information Services Division, Federal Bureau of Investigation. https://ucr.fbi.gov/crime-in-the-u.s/2019/crime-in-the-u.s.-2019/additional-data-collections/humantrafficking/human-trafficking.pdf

U.S. Department of Homeland Security. (n.d.). *Myths and misconceptions.* https://www.dhs.gov/Blue-campaign/myths-and-misconceptions

U.S. Department of State. (2020, June). *Trafficking in person report*, 20th ed. https://www.state.gov/wp-content/uploads/2020/06/2020-TIP-Report-Complete-062420-FINAL.pdf

Viuhko, M. (2010, Jan). Human trafficking for sexual exploitation and organized procuring in Finland. *European Journal of Criminology, 7*(1), 61–75.

Wells, M., Mitchell, K. J., & Ji, K. (2012, May). Exploring the role of the internet in juvenile prostitution cases coming to the attention of law enforcement. *Journal of Child Sexual Abuse: Research, Treatment, & Program Innovations for Victims, Survivors, & Offenders, 21*(3), 327–342.

Wiener, R. L., Berry, M. C., Wertheimer, J., Petty, T., & Martinez, J. (2021, May). The public's judgement of sex trafficked women: Blaming the victim? *Journal of Experimental Psychology: Applied.*

Wilson, B. (2019, March). Global problem, local solutions: Challenges to exiting commercial sexual exploitation and service provision. *International Social Work, 62*(2), 741–753.

Wilson, B., & Butler, L. D. (2014, September). Running a gauntlet: A review of victimization and violence in the pre-entry, post-entry, and peri-/post-exit periods of commercial sexual exploitation. *Psychological Trauma: Theory, Research, Practice, and Policy, 6*(5), 494–504.

# Chapter 2
# Legal Aspects

**Abstract** This chapter provides an overview of the history of the laws and legislation pertaining to sex trafficking, both domestically and internationally. The history of domestic and international laws on sex trafficking has evolved over the years. Through federal initiatives, the Trafficking Victims Protection Act (TVPA) was established, and a shift was made to utilize anti-trafficking law enforcement and assistance programs. Legislature was implemented to protect victims of sex trafficking and to aid in successful prosecution of traffickers. The creation and refinement of some of the most influential laws are summarized. Data collection by the US Trafficking in Persons Report and the UN Global Report on Trafficking in Persons, as well as other sources, are presented to examine governmental systematic efforts to track the rates of sex trafficking. Based on the review, some important factors that are consistently related to sex trafficking include corruption within different legal systems and legalized sex work. Following the general overview of the legal aspects, this brief chapter will discuss specific legal issues for human trafficking.

**Keywords** Law · Policy · Legislation

## 2.1 Introduction

In the year 2000, human trafficking became a focus of national attention in the United States, although the issue of human trafficking was rooted and derived from the US Constitution, which stated "neither slavery nor involuntary servitude, except as a punishment for crime whereof the party shall have been duly convicted, shall exist within the United States, or any place subject to their jurisdiction" (U.S. Const. art. XIII, § 1). With the enactment of the Trafficking Victims Protection Act of 2000 (TVPA), the United States developed a national framework and response to combat and eliminate modern forms of slavery (e.g., commercial sex industry, modern slavery, forced labor) including both domestic and international. The establishment of the TVPA (2000) acknowledged human trafficking as criminal behavior and provided a legal framework for the prosecution of traffickers. The development of

 
J. Davidtz et al., *Sex Trafficking*, SpringerBriefs in Psychology,
https://doi.org/10.1007/978-3-031-09120-9_2

human trafficking laws and legislation over the past two decades have led to a variety of responses to modern slavery and human trafficking (e.g., prevention, awareness, support), which are often rooted in local statutory or voluntary services (Gardner et al., 2021).

## 2.2 Relevant Laws and Legislation

### *2.2.1 Domestic*

The Trafficking Victims Protection Act of 2000, as amended (TVPA, 2000), defined severe forms of trafficking in persons as:

> Sex trafficking in which a commercial sex act is induced by force, fraud, or coercion in which the person induced to perform such act has not attained 18 years of age; or the recruitment, harboring, transportation, provision, or obtaining of a person for labor or services, through the use of force, fraud, or coercion for the purpose of subjection to involuntary servitude, peonage, debt bondage, or slavery.

The TVPA (2000) was the first comprehensive federal law to address human trafficking and provided a three-pronged approach (prevention, protection, and prosecution). The TVPA strengthened the US prevention efforts by providing and establishing international initiatives to improve opportunities for human trafficking survivors (e.g., created the Office to Monitor and Combat Trafficking in Persons in the State Department). The TVPA increased protections for human trafficking survivors in the United States (e.g., foreign survivors are eligible for federally funded benefits/services – regardless of immigration status, protection from removal for victims of trafficking (the T visa) and victims of certain crimes (the U visa). Lastly, the TVPA enhanced the capacity of federal prosecutor to bring human traffickers to justice for their crimes (e.g., criminalizing behaviors, mandating restitution, providing forfeiture, and strengthening penalties).

Over the past two decades, the TVPA has been amended and reauthorized multiple times to provide further assistance in combating the issue of human trafficking. Key changes are subsequently listed. The Trafficking Victims Protection Reauthorization Act of 2003 (TVPRA, 2003) added provisions to disseminate materials about the illegal nature of sex tourism, created civil actions for trafficking survivors to sue their trafficker, and required the Attorney General to report annual anti-trafficking efforts. The TVPRA (2005) emphasized the protection of human trafficking survivors who resided in the United States, which included grant programs, victim assistance programs, and the creation of comprehensive service/rehabilitative facilities. The TVPRA (2008) extended and modified certain programs from the Department of Justice, the Department of Labor, and the Department of Health and Human Services. These provisions (a) included the imposition of penalties on those who obstructed investigations, (b) changed the standard of proof (the government only has to prove that the defendant acted in a "reckless disregard of the fact, such means [force, fraud, or coercion] would be used"), (c) eliminated the requirement that the defendant knew the survivor was a minor, and (d) imposed criminal liability on those who intend to defraud or recruit workers from outside the United States and established protection laws for unaccompanied alien minors.

The TVPRA (2013) was passed as an amendment to the Violence Against Women Act, prevented child marriages, and strengthened the collaboration with state and local law enforcement to charge and prosecute traffickers. The TVPRA (2015) stated that the use of direct assets seized in trafficking crimes could be used to fund victim restitution and directed the Attorney General to create and maintain a National Strategy to Combat Human Trafficking. The TVPRA (2017) included the training of school resource officers and training for school personnel on human trafficking. Also, they increased government efforts to eliminate human trafficking via concrete actions: enforcement actions taken, investigations actively underway, prosecutions conducted, convictions attained, training provided, programs and partnerships actively underway, efforts to prevent severe forms of trafficking (e.g., programs to reduce the vulnerability of populations, involve survivors in community engagement and policy-making), and victim services offered (e.g., immigration services and restitution). More recently, the TVPA (2019) amended that governments (i.e., policy) can also act as traffickers of human trafficking in government-funded programs.

Historically, children who were recognized as a victim of a crime under both state and federal laws were arrested and convicted of prostitution (Polaris Project, 2015). In 2009, the State of Washington implemented the first Safe Harbor Law. These laws were developed by States to address inconsistencies with how children were exploited for commercial sex and sex trafficking (i.e., prostituted minors) (Green et al., 2019). Additionally, the core elements of Safe Harbor Laws include legal protection (i.e., immunity, diversion) and provisions of services (i.e., mandatory referral – medical, psychological, housing, education, job training, and language and legal assistance; Polaris Project, 2015; Green et al., 2019). Safe Harbor Laws were implemented to redirect youth away from the justice system. Thus, federal law indicated that a child under the age of 18 and is induced into providing commercial sex is a survivor of trafficking and must be treated as such (Clayton et al., 2013). Furthermore, the Uniform Act on Prevention of and Remedies for Human Trafficking (Section 15) stated an immunity of a minor includes "an individual who was a minor at the time of the offense is not criminally liable or subject to [juvenile delinquency proceeding] for [prostitution] and [insert other non-violent offenses] committed as a direct result of being a victim of human trafficking" (National Conference of Commissioners on Uniform State Laws, 2013). However, in some communities, juveniles continue to be arrested and incarcerated for prostitution-related charges or "masking" charges because of misidentification (Halter, 2010; Mitchell et al., 2013; Reid & Jones, 2011; Smith et al., 2009).

Moreover, the United States implemented additional laws and acts to combat human trafficking and provide more services and support to human trafficking survivors. The Preventing Sex Trafficking and Strengthening Families Act (2014) provided changes to existing laws regarding the child welfare system (e.g., areas of foster parenting, adoption incentive payments). Additionally, it required data collection, screening of children who may be at high risk, and reporting of sex trafficking incidents and develops protocols for locating missing or runaway children. Primarily, it sought to reduce the number of incidences of sex trafficking survivors of individuals involved in the foster care system.

The TVPA initiated and transformed the evolution of combating human trafficking. With each subsequent TVPRA, there was a shift from international trafficking and funding services/support for immigrant survivors in the United States to domestic survivors and those trafficked for sexual exploitation (United Nations Office on Drugs and Crime [UNODC], 2020). Despite evolving rules, laws, and policies, there is a dearth of research on the effectiveness of anti-trafficking policies (Goździak & Bump, 2008), and the studies that do exist primarily focus on the effectiveness of the federal trafficking statute. Even though there are federal and state legislations addressing human trafficking, the ability to successfully identify victims remains a challenge (Farrell & Pfeffer, 2014; Okech et al., 2012). Likewise, it has caused similar challenges in regard to human trafficking arrests, charges, and convictions, which subsequently have caused doubt among some on the magnitude of the problem (UNODC, 2008).

### 2.2.2 *International*

International law "consists of rules and principles governing the relations and dealings of nations with each other, as well as the relations between states and individuals, and relations between international organizations" (Cornell Law School, n.d.). Human trafficking is an international problem; thus, in a legal context, it is frequently used interchangeably with the concept of slavery and "slave-like" practices (i.e., peonage, involuntary servitude, bonded labor, forced labor) (Office of Justice Programs, n.d.). International law is prevalent in regard to human trafficking cases, as crimes may occur across borders and/or the trafficker(s) or survivor(s) may have originated from different countries. The intersection across multiple jurisdictions (United States) and/or other countries may complicate the legal process as each country may have its own human trafficking laws (Office of Justice Programs, n.d.).

In a prevailing manner to combat human trafficking, the United Nations Convention against Transnational Organized Crime, in 2000, approved the Protocol to Prevent, Suppress, and Punish Trafficking Persons, known as the UN Trafficking in Person Protocol or "Palermo Protocol" (Protocol to Prevent, 2000). The Palermo Protocol was the first legally binding instrument to aid in the detection and exploitation of human trafficking with an internationally recognized definition of human trafficking (UNODC, 2004). The Palermo Protocol was defined as the protocol to prevent, suppress, and punish traffickers (Protocol to Prevent, 2000). Any country that ratified the Palermo Protocol Treaty must criminalize human trafficking and develop anti-trafficking laws distinguished in the protocols' legal provisions and provide protection and assistance to human trafficking survivors (Protocol to

Prevent, 2000). Then in 2003, the United Nations adopted Palermo Protocol, which included three components:

1. The Protocol to Prevent, Suppress and Punish Trafficking in Persons, especially Women and Children (i.e., facilitate convergence in national approaches and support international cooperation in investigations and prosecutions of traffickers).
2. The Protocol against the Smuggling of Migrants by Land, Sea and Air (i.e., defined smuggling of migrants and aimed to prevent, combat, the smuggling of migrants).
3. The Protocol against the Illicit Manufacturing and Trafficking in Firearms, Their Parts and Components and Ammunition (i.e., promote, facilitate, and strengthen cooperation between States, in order to prevent, combat, and eradicate the illicit manufacturing of and trafficking in firearms) (UNODC, 2004).

Since the implementation of the Palermo Protocol, it has reached almost universal ratification, totaling 178 parties, and enhanced the capacity to detect, prosecute, and prevent human trafficking across the entire international community (U.S. Department of State, 2021).

According to the European Commission (2018), human trafficking is prohibited by the European Union Charter of Fundamental Rights (*Article 5*), with links to the immigration policy (*Article 79*), and is considered a serious form of organized crime by the Treaty of the Functioning of the European Union (*Article 83*). Human trafficking policies and the legal framework of the European Union are considered to be victim-centered, gender-specific, and child-sensitive and anchored in human rights (European Commission, n.d.). This is consistent with the European Union Anti-trafficking Directive, a legislative act which addressed human trafficking, established minimum rules, defined criminal offences and sanctions, and strengthened victim protection, assistance, support, and prevention and important figures to fight against human trafficking (Preventing and Combating, 2011). Herein, the Anti-trafficking Directive included three constitutive elements of human trafficking: acts (i.e., consists of recruitment, transportation, harboring or receiving of persons), means (i.e., way in which control is attained – threat, use of force, coercion, abduction, fraud, deception, abuse of power), and purpose (i.e., exploitation of trafficked survivor – prostitution, sexual exploitation, forced labor, begging, slavery) (European Commission, 2020).

Following the directive policy on human trafficking came the European Union's Strategy towards the Eradication of Trafficking in Human Beings 2012–2016. This strategy set the policy framework and identified five priorities: (a) identifying, protecting, and assisting victims of human trafficking, (b) increasing the prevention of human trafficking, (c) improving the prosecution of trafficker, (d) enhancing the coordination and cooperation among institution actors, and (e) increasing the knowledge and effectiveness of human trafficking concerns (European Commissioner, n.d.). More recently, the European Union adopted new strategies to combat human trafficking and includes providing a comprehensive response to the crime, from preventing the crime, and protecting and empowering survivors to bring their traffickers to justice (European Commission, 2021). As of 2020, a total of 169 out of 181 counties assessed in the Global Report on Trafficking in Persons have legislation that criminalizes human trafficking broadly in line with the Palermo Protocol (U.S. Department of State, 2021).

## 2.3 Governmental Systemic Efforts to Track Rates

### *2.3.1 United Nations Global Report on Trafficking in Persons*

The Global Report on Trafficking in Persons was mandated by the United Nation's General Assembly in 2010 for the Global Plan of Action to Combat Trafficking in Persons (UNODC, 2020).Thus, the first United Nations Global Report on Trafficking in Persons was published in 2012, and it provided an overview of human trafficking patterns at a global, regional, and national level. Previous reports have offered an assessment of the scope of human trafficking, including what has been done to combat it, and provided an overview of human trafficking patterns, legal actions, and country-specific information on reported cases of human trafficking survivors and prosecutors (UNODC, 2020). In total, there have been five published reports, with the most recent report published in 2020. The most recent report covered a total of 148 countries and provided an overview of human trafficking patterns and flows at a global, regional, and national level, from cases detected between 2016 and 2019 (UNODC, 2020). For example, the report provided information on socioeconomic conditions used by traffickers to recruit and exploit survivors; patterns of child tracking – roles of extreme poverty, social norms, and familial backgrounds; forced labor and economic sectors; and technology Internet patterns used to facilitate recruitment and exploitation (UNODC, 2020). The aims and goals of these reports were to assist governments, parliaments, and stakeholders with developing solutions to address the causes and risk factors of human trafficking, prosecuting offenders, protecting the vulnerable, and better supporting victims (UNODC, 2020).

### *2.3.2 US Trafficking in Persons Report*

The Trafficking in Persons Report (TIPS) is federally mandated by the US Department of State. The Department of State leads the US global engagement to combat human trafficking and supports the coordination of anti-trafficking efforts across the US government (U.S. Department of State, 2021). In 2002, a National Security Presidential Directive 22 (National Security, 2002), on combating trafficking in persons (i.e., instructions for federal agencies to strengthen collective efforts, capabilities, and coordination to support the policy to combat human trafficking) and an executive order for the President's Interagency Task Force to Monitor and

Combat Trafficking in Persons (Exec. Order No. 13257, 2002), was implemented. The **Office to Monitor and Combat Trafficking in Persons collaborated with** foreign governments, international organizations, federal agencies, civil societies, private sectors, and survivors of human trafficking to combat human trafficking (U.S. Department of State, 2021). They used information from the US embassies, government officials, and nongovernmental and international organizations and published reports, news articles, academic studies, consultations with authorities and organizations, and information submitted to TIPS via email (U.S. Department of State, 2021). For example, the 2021 TIPS covers government efforts across the world from April 1, 2020, through March 31, 2021. The United States follows the "3P" paradigm, prosecution, protection, and prevention, to combat human trafficking worldwide. The US Department of State (2021) ranked governments based on their perceived efforts to acknowledge and combat human trafficking by placing each country onto one of four ties. The tier placement is based on the country's extent of government efforts to meet the TVPA's minimum standards for the elimination of human trafficking:

1. The government should prohibit severe forms of human trafficking and punish the acts.
2. The knowing commission of any act of sex trafficking involving force, fraud, coercion or in which the survivor of sex trafficking is a child incapable of giving consent, rape, kidnapping, or death, the government should advise punishment commensurate the crime.
3. The knowing commission of any act of a severe form of human trafficking, the government should prescribe punishment that is sufficiently stringent to deter and reflect the heinous nature of the offense.
4. The government should make serious and sustained efforts to eliminate severe forms of human trafficking (TVPA, 2000).

A Tier 1 ranking is the highest; however, that does not mean that a country does not have a human trafficking problem or that they are doing enough to address the crime. Rather, a Tier 1 ranking indicated that a country's government had made efforts to address the problem of human trafficking and meet the TVPA's minim standards. In order to maintain a Tier 1 ranking, the country's government has to demonstrate appreciable progress each year to combat human trafficking (U.S. Department of State, 2021). A description of the tiers is provided:

1. Tier 1: Country governments fully meet the TVPA's minimum standards for the elimination of human trafficking.
2. Tier 2: Countries whose governments do not fully meet the TVPA's minimum standards but are making significant efforts to become compliant with those standards.
3. Tier 2 Watch List: Countries whose governments do not fully meet the TVPA's minimum standards but are making significant efforts to become compliant with those standards, for example, the estimated number of survivors of human trafficking is very significant or is significantly increasing, and the country is not

taking actions, or there is a failure to provide evidence of increasing efforts to combat human trafficking from the previous year.

4. Tier 3: Countries whose governments do not fully meet the TVPA's minimum standards and are not making significant efforts to do so (U.S. Department of State, 2021).

The TIPS is the most comprehensive worldwide report on government's efforts to combat human trafficking (U.S. Department of State, 2021). Although the TIPS provided an abundance of useful and prevalent information, it is imperfect in the sense that its statistics and rankings are based on country's nongovernment officials and provide their government reports with data; thus, the data cannot be independently verified (U.S. Department of State, 2021).

## 2.4 The Role of Legal Corruption

Corruption is identified as "the abuse of entrusted power for private gain" (Transparency International, n.d.). Corruption has a wide range of corrosive effects, undermines democracy and laws, and leads to violations of human rights, quality of life, organized crime, terrorism, and threats to human security (International Bar Association, 2016). People who live in countries plagued by poverty, gender inequality, high crime, war, and corruption are at higher risks of human trafficking (Clawson et al., 2006) and, moreover, higher risks of victimization and corruption because weak institutions offer weak protection (Transparency International, n.d.). Furthermore, corruption among government agencies/authorities undermine the efforts to investigate, prosecute, and convict traffickers (International Bar Association, 2016). Corruption plays a role in every stage of the human trafficking process (i.e., initial planning to trafficking), and exploitation begins (UNODC, 2011). The UNODC (2011) reported that public officials are most vulnerable to corruption in relation to human trafficking, 65% of the respondents indicated border control/immigration/customs, 50% indicated law enforcement and police, and 25% considered civil society organizations. Moreover, the connection between corruption and human trafficking is considered a "high-profit-low-risk venture," whereas the traffickers have sizeable monetary gains to the limited risk of getting caught and being brought to trail (Transparency International, n.d.). Lastly, corruption reinforces human trafficking in four ways: (a) allows human trafficking to remain invisible, (b) facilitates impunity even if trafficking is detected, (c) facilitates trafficking circuits in the country, and (d) increases the danger of revictimization (International Bar Association, 2016, as cited in IACC Workshop Summary).

Public officials have directly participated in human trafficking by playing an active role in the recruitment, transportation, and exploitation (Transparency International, n.d.; UNODC, 2011). Moreover, due to public official's close proximity to vulnerable populations, it allows them to target potential human trafficking survivors (International Bar Association, 2016). Corruption in the recruitment phase of human trafficking is "likely to take the form of buying the silence of government bodies that are responsible for protecting society from such duplicitous actions" (Transparency International, n.d.). Corruption in the transportation phase of human trafficking often occurs during border crossings, and the transit points of entry often involve law enforcement or other public officials (Transparency International, n.d.). Corruption in the exploitation phase of human trafficking often occurs when raids or arrests happen and traffickers pay of law enforcement officers, prosecutors, or judges to drop the charges (Transparency International, n.d.). Corrupt officials facilitated exemption by obstructing the detection, investigation, prosecution, and punishment of traffickers, through facilitation which included ignoring human trafficking red flags, protecting traffickers, refusing to register human trafficking complaints, notifying human traffickers of law enforcement operations, providing security to human trafficking operations, obstructing investigations, obstructing prosecutions, and reducing punishments (International Bar Association, 2016).

The UNODC's Convention Against Corruption (2004) provided preventative policies for human trafficking directed at public and private sectors. These policies included the establishment of anti-corruption (e.g., enhance transparency in finances and political campaigns); public services are subject to safeguards (e.g., promote efficiency, transparency, and recruitment); public officials should be subjected to codes of conduct, financial disclosures, and disciplinary measures; and transparency and accountability (UNODC, 2011). The UNODC (2011) identified problem areas with anti-trafficking and anti-corruption approaches, which included:

1. Traffickers may recruit, transport, and exploit their victims due to corruption.
2. Lack of investigation, prosecution, and adjudication of human trafficking due to corruption.
3. Lack of information and data collection on human trafficking-related corruption.
4. Protection of human trafficking survivors impeded by corrupt public officials.
5. Lack of adequate responses to causes of human trafficking.
6. Lack of adequate responses against major impediments to adequate criminal justice response.

Lastly, the UNODC (2011) provided recommendations to help combat the aforementioned issues of corruption in human trafficking:

- Streamlining approaches.
- Connecting relevant actors.
- Identification of vulnerable sectors.
- Awareness-raising and training of relevant public officials.
- Ensuring transparency of performance.
- Developing and implementing codes of conduct for law enforcement agencies, criminal justice actors, and international civil servants.
- Establishment of control mechanisms.
- Disciplinary and judicial responses.
- Personnel recruitment and training.
- Cooperation between anti-trafficking and anti-corruption practitioners.

- Improvement of data collection.
- Improvement of protection of victims of trafficking who report corruption.
- Involving civil society and the private sector.
- Incentives and protection measures.
- Developing joint strategies.

## 2.5 Criminalization Versus Decriminalization of Sex Work/ Prostitution

Legalized sex work and prostitution are controversial in nature, and arguments have been made on whether they should be decriminalized and how they relate to sex trafficking/human trafficking. According to Albright and D'Adamo (2017), the criminalization of prostitution leads to increased violence, erosion of trust, increased vulnerability, and stigma: first, increased violence due to the fact that prostitution is regarded as criminal activity and thus easy targets for abuse and exploitation; second, erosion of trust within support systems (i.e., healthcare) out of fear of judgment, discrimination, lower quality of service, and/or legal consequences; third, increased vulnerability due to consequences of involvement in the criminal justice system (e.g., arrest, conviction, difficulty finding housing and employment); and, finally, stigma reinforced through criminalization, which perpetuates sex worker's marginalization. The criminalization of sex work increases sex workers' vulnerability to violence, exploitation, and human trafficking (Albright & D'Adamo, 2017). In contrast, arguments for the decriminalization of prostitution support the recognition of sex workers' human rights, which is a critical mechanism for decreasing human trafficking (Amnesty International, 2016). Additionally, the decriminalization of sex work allows sex workers who experience violence to seek help from law enforcement and healthcare workers without the fear of consequences for themselves or others (Albright & D'Adamo, 2017). The decriminalization will allow businesses to recruit among domestic women who choose sex work as their free choice of occupation, which will make resorting to human trafficking survivors less attractive (Segrave, 2009). Lastly, those who freely choose sex work noted policies should focus on improving sex workers' working conditions and provide social protection (Lim, 2007). Overall, research in relation to human trafficking found that countries where prostitution is legal experience large report of human trafficking cases (Fox, 2021 & Farley, 2009).

## 2.6 Legal Issues

The first time individuals who have survived human trafficking come into contact with law enforcement are often as the offender and not as the victim (Clawson & Dutch, 2006; Emerson, 2019). Human trafficking survivors are commonly arrested for prostitution and other crimes (i.e., possession of weapons, drugs, or identity theft) which have been orchestrated by their trafficker (Polaris Project, 2019). Historically, law enforcement officers have struggled with identifying human trafficking survivors (Clawson et al., 2006; Farrell et al., 2008; Farrell et al., 2014; Farrell et al., 2015; Farrell & Pfeffer, 2014). Law enforcement officers cannot accurately identify human trafficking incidents in their communities; then human trafficking survivors will be denied legal justice as their perpetrators will not be investigated, charged, and convicted (Barrick et al., 2020). Law enforcements face many challenges when trying to identify these victims including overcoming trafficking techniques such as coercion, online solicitation, hidden venues, interstate movement, as well as issues with police reporting and investigations (Nichols & Heil, 2014). Human trafficking victims may not disclose information due to fear of punishment, lack of incentive to testify, lengthy and stressful judicial procedures, and distrust in the legal system (Constantinou, 2016). Without the survivor's willingness and cooperation, law enforcement officers have difficulty building cases against the trafficker which hinders their ability to prevent them from victimizing other people. A survivor of human trafficking may feel afraid to press charges if they do not identify as a victim or assume blame for their situation (DeBoise, 2014; National Institute of Justice, 2016; Constantinou, 2016). This is a critical point in an investigation where law enforcement must demonstrate empathy to connect with the survivor and offer resources within the community. Lack of survivor cooperation was the most frequently reported challenge (70%) experienced by law enforcement during investigations, and little information exists on the type of education and training investigators are receiving (Farrell et al., 2008).

## References


Albright, E., & D'Adamo, K. (2017). Decreasing human trafficking through sex work decriminalization. *AMA Journal of Ethics, 19*(1), 122–126. https://doi.org/10.1001/journalofethics.2017.19.1.sect2-1701

Amnesty International. (2016). *Sex workers at risk: A research summary on human rights abuses against sex workers.* https://www.amnestyusa.org/files/briefing_-_sex_workers_rights_-_embargoed_-_final.pdf

Barrick, K., Panichelli, M., Lambdin, B., Dang, M., & Lutnick, A. (2020). Law enforcement identification of potential trafficking victims. *Journal of Crime and Justice.* https://doi.org/10.1080/0735648X.2020.1837204

Clawson, H., & Dutch, N. (2006). *Identifying victims of human trafficking: Inherent challenges and promising strategies from the field.* https://aspe.hhs.gov/sites/default/files/migrated_legacy_files//42671/ib.pdf

Clawson, H., Dutch, N., & Cummings, M. (2006). *Law enforcement response to human trafficking and implications for victims: Current practices and lessons learned.* http://www.ojp.usdoj.gov/nij

Clayton, E. W., Krugman, R. D., & Simon, P. (2013). *Confronting commercial sexual exploitation and sex trafficking of minors in the United States.*

Constantinou, A. (2016). Is crime displacement inevitable? Lessons from the enforcement of laws against prostitution-related human trafficking in Cyprus. *European Journal of Criminology., 13*(2), 214–230.

Cornell Law School. (n.d.). *International law*. https://www.law.cornell.edu/wex/international_law

DeBoise, C. (2014). Human trafficking and sex work: Foundational social-work principles. *Meridians, 12*(1), 227–233. https://doi.org/10.2979/meridians.12.1.227

Emerson, J. (2019). *State report cards: grading criminal record relief laws for survivors of human trafficking*. https://scholarworks.law.ubalt.edu/all_fac/1079

European Commission. (n.d.). *Together against trafficking in human beings*. European Commission. https://ec.europa.eu/anti-trafficking/legal-and-policy-framework_en

European Commission. (2018). *Working together to address trafficking in human beings*. https://ec.europa.eu/anti-trafficking/system/files/2018-12/key_concepts_in_a_nutshell.pdf

European Commission. (2020). *Study on the economic, social and human costs of trafficking in human beings within the EU*. European Commission. https://ec.europa.eu/anti-trafficking/system/files/2020-10/study_on_the_economic_social_and_human_costs_of_trafficking_in_human_beings_within_the_eu.pdf

European Commission. (2021). *Communication from the commission to the European parliament, the council, the European economic and social committee and the committee of the regions empty*. https://eur-lex.europa.eu/legal-content/EN/TXT/?uri=CELEX:52021DC0171

Exec. Order No. 13257, 3 C.F.R. 7259–7260. (2002). https://www.federalregister.gov/documents/2002/02/19/02-4071/presidents-interagency-task-force-to-monitor-and-combat-trafficking-in-persons

Farley, M. (2009). Theory versus reality: Commentary on four articles about trafficking for prostitution. *Women's Studies International Forum, 32*(4), 311–315.

Farrell, A., McDevitt, J., & Fahy, S. (2008). *Understanding and improving law enforcement responses to human trafficking (Final report Grant No. 2005-IJ-CX-0045, submitted to National Institute of Justice, U.S. Department of Justice, Washington, DC)*. Northeastern University. https://www.ncjrs.gov/pdffiles1/nij/grants/222752.pdf

Farrell, A., Owens, C., & McDevitt, J. (2014). New laws but few cases: Understanding the challenges to the investigation and prosecution of human trafficking cases. *Crime, Law and Social Change, 61*, 139–168. https://doi.org/10.1007/s10611-013-9442-1

Farrell, A., & Pfeffer, R. (2014). Policing human trafficking: Cultural blinders and organizational barriers. *Annals of the American Academy of Political and Social Science, 653*(1), 46–64.

Farrell, A., Pfeffer, R., & Bright, K. (2015). Police perceptions of human trafficking. *Journal of Crime and Justice*. https://doi.org/10.1080/0735648X.2014.995412

Fox, J. (2021). International law after dark: How legalized sex work can comport with international and human rights law. *Chicago Journal of International Law, 22*(1), 16.

Gardner, A., Northall, P., & Brewster, B. (2021). Building slavery free communities: A resilience framework. *Journal of Human Trafficking, 7*(3), 338–353. https://doi.org/10.1080/23322705.2020.1777828

Goździak, E., & Bump, M. (2008). *Data and research on human trafficking: Bibliography of research-based literature*.

Green, B., Gies, S., Healy, E., & Bobnis, A. (2019). *Safe harbor laws: Changing the legal response to minors involved in commercial sex, phase 3, the qualitative analysis*. https://www.ojp.gov/pdffiles1/ojjdp/grants/253244.pdf

Halter, S. (2010). Factors that influence police conceptualizations of girls involved in prostitution in six U.S. cities: Child sexual exploitation victims or delinquents? *Child Maltreatment, 15*(2), 152–160. https://doi.org/10.1177/1077559509355315

International Bar Association. (2016). *Human trafficking and public corruption, a report by the IBA's presidential task force against human trafficking*. https://www.ibanet.org/MediaHandler?id=E34FFA1D-8038-4AEC-A631-E0E2A7E0AD86

Lim, L. L. (2007). *Trafficking, demand and the sex market*. Paper presented at the International Symposium on Gender at the Heart of Globalization, Paris. https://documentation.lastradain-

ternational.org/lsidocs/334%20Lin%20Lean%20Lim%20TraffickingDemand%20Sex%20market.pdf
Mitchell, K. J., Finkelhor, D. & Wolak, J. (2013). Sex trafficking cases involving minors. (2013). *Crimes against Children Research Center*, University of New Hampshire: Durham, NH.
National Conference of Commissioners on Uniform State Laws. (2013). *Uniform act on prevention of and remedies for human trafficking*. https://www.uniformlaws.org/HigherLogic/System/DownloadDocumentFile.ashx?DocumentFileKey=bf446992-1305-1676-c59f-eb0b7f1f9ef1&forceDialog=0
National Institute of Justice. (2016). *Improving the investigation and prosecution of state and local human trafficking cases*. http://nij.gov/topics/crime/human-trafficking/pages/improving-investigation-and-prosecution-of-human-trafficking-cases.aspx
National Security Presidential Directive 22. (2002). *Trafficking in persons*. https://ctip.defense.gov/Portals/12/Documents/NSPD-22.pdf
Nichols, A. J., & Heil, E. C. (2014). Challenges to identifying and prosecuting sex trafficking cases in the Midwest United States. *Feminist Criminology, 10*(1), 7–35. https://doi.org/10.1177/1557085113519490
Office of Justice Programs. (n.d.). *Human trafficking task force e-guide*. https://www.ovcttac.gov/taskforceguide/eguide/1-understanding-human-trafficking/14-human-trafficking-laws/international-law/
Okech, D., Morreau, W., & Benson, K. (2012). Human trafficking: Improving victim identification and service provision. *International Social Work, 55*(4), 488–503.
Polaris Project. (2015). *Human trafficking issue brief: Safe harbor.* https://polarisproject.org/wp-content/uploads/2019/09/2015-Safe-Harbor-Issue-Brief.pdf
Polaris Project. (2019). *The importance of criminal record relief for human trafficking survivors*. https://polarisproject.org/blog/2019/03/the-importance-of-criminal-record-relief-for-human-trafficking-survivors/
Preventing and Combating Trafficking in Human Beings and Protecting its Victims, April 5. 2011. https://eur-lex.europa.eu/LexUriServ/LexUriServ.do?uri=OJ:L:2011:101:0001:0011:EN:PDF
Preventing Sex Trafficking and Strengthening Families Act (2014). Pub. L. No. 113–183.
Protocol to Prevent, Suppress and Punish Trafficking in Persons Especially Women and Children, supplementing the United Nations Convention against Transnational Organized Crime, November 15, 2000. https://www.ohchr.org/en/professionalinterest/pages/protocoltraffickinginpersons.aspx
Reid, J. A., & Jones, S. (2011). Exploited vulnerability: Legal and psychological perspectives on child sex trafficking victims. *Victims & Offenders, 6*(2), 207–231.
Segrave, M. (2009). Order at the border: The repatriation of victims of trafficking. *Women's Studies International Forum, 32*(4), 251–260.
Smith, L., Vardaman, S. H., & Snow, M. (2009). *The national report on domestic minor sex trafficking: America's prostituted children*.
Trafficking Victims Protection ACT of 2000. (2000). Pub. L. No. 106–386.
Trafficking Victims Protection Reauthorization Act of 2003. (2003). Pub. L. No. 108–193, 117 Stat. 2875.
Trafficking Victims Protection Reauthorization Act of 2005 (2005). Pub. L. No. 109–164, 119 Stat. 3558.
Trafficking Victims Protection Reauthorization Act of 2008 (2008). Pub. L. No. 110–457, 122 Stat. 5055.
Trafficking Victims Protection Reauthorization Act of 2013 (2013). Pub. L. No. 113–4.
Trafficking Victims Protection Reauthorization Act of 2015 (2015). Pub. L. No. 114–22.
Trafficking Victims Protection Reauthorization Act of 2017 (2017). Pub. L. No. 115–427.
Trafficking Victims Protection Reauthorization Act of 2019. (2019). Pub. L. No. 115–425.
Transparency International the Global Coalition against Corruption. (n.d.) *What is corruption?* https://www.transparency.org/en/what-is-corruption

United Nations Office on Drugs and Crime. (2004). *United nations convention against transnational organized crime and the protocols thereto.* https://www.unodc.org/documents/treaties/UNTOC/Publications/TOC%20Convention/TOCebook-e.pdf

United Nations Office on Drugs and Crime. (2008). *An introduction to human trafficking: Vulnerability, impact, and action.* https://www.unodc.org/documents/human-trafficking/An_Introduction_to_Human_Trafficking_-_Background_Paper.pdf

United Nations Office on Drugs and Crime. (2011). *Issue paper, the role of corruption in trafficking in persons.* https://www.unodc.org/documents/human-trafficking/2011/Issue_Paper_-_The_Role_of_Corruption_in_Trafficking_in_Persons.pdf

United Nations Office on Drugs and Crime. (2020). *Global report on trafficking in persons 2020.* https://www.unodc.org/documents/data-and-analysis/tip/2021/GLOTiP_2020_15jan_web.pdf

U.S. Const. art. XIII, § 1.

U.S. Department of State. (2021). *2021 trafficking in persons report.* https://www.state.gov/wp-content/uploads/2021/09/TIPR-GPA-upload-07222021.pdf

# Chapter 3
# Assessments and Measures

**Abstract** In this chapter examines the available screening tools and measures pertaining to identification and needs of survivors of sex trafficking. Assessments and measures include objective measures, interviews, screening tools, and trauma-informed approaches. This chapter will conclude with considerations and recommendations for the development of future assessments and measures that are survivor-centered and clinically relevant. Assessments will be discussed in clinical and forensic contexts when appropriate.

**Keywords** Sex trafficking victims · Screening tool · Identification · Assessment · Measure

## 3.1 Introduction

Over the past two decades, there has been a global increase of evidence-based research on the identification of survivors, as well as the needs and associated issues that survivors of sex trafficking experience (Romero et al., 2021; Graham et al., 2019; Macy & Graham, 2012). Some of the most prevalent risk factors for sex trafficking put forth in the literature include vulnerable populations (e.g., low-income women, LGBTQ+ individuals, individuals of color), a history of involvement in the child welfare system, substance use or mental health concerns, a history of running away or homelessness, being sexually abused or victimized as a child, as well as presenting in emergency medical settings (Haney et al., 2020; Lockyer, 2020; Chisolm-Straker et al., 2019). Most individuals who survive sex trafficking report interacting with healthcare and other clinical professionals, however; many of these individuals go unidentified, and as such, their needs are not fully understood (Marcinkowski et al., 2022; Kennedy et al., 2021).

 
J. Davidtz et al., *Sex Trafficking*, SpringerBriefs in Psychology,
https://doi.org/10.1007/978-3-031-09120-9_3

## 3.2 Identifying Victims of Sex Trafficking

Identification is a necessary first step before aiding individuals who have survived sex trafficking. While many challenges present themselves when attempting to identify these individuals, providers can familiarize themselves with known indicators to better recognize the signs. Providers in a variety of settings including hospitals, emergency departments, private practices, and school counseling and forensic settings may benefit from learning these indicators (Browne-James et al., 2021; Greenbaum et al., 2018; Macy & Graham, 2012). As initially discussed in Chap. 1, it is also imperative that counselors, clinicians, and various other providers who encounter those who experience sex trafficking are educated on commonly held myths and misconceptions (Franklin & Menaker, 2015; Haney et al., 2020; Rajaram & Tidball, 2018; Wiener et al., 2021), as well as strategies that promote the identification of individuals who have survived or are currently experiencing sex trafficking. Individuals often go unidentified and may choose not to self-report victimization due to a multitude of reasons including (a) fear of disclosure (Barnert et al., 2019), (b) not viewing themselves as victims or in need of help (Rafferty, 2016), and (c) the power, control, and grooming techniques imposed by their trafficker (Reid & Jones, 2011).

A systematic review conducted by Macy and Graham (2012) synthesized service identification recommendations for agencies and practitioners that work with individuals who have survived trafficking. Primary indicators of sex trafficking include signs (a) of physical abuse, (b) the person is under the control of another person, (c) signs the person is unable to move or leave a job, and (d) the person is depressed or fearful. All these indicators were also previously published by the US Department of Health and Human Services (2008). Strategies for providers to implement while working directly with potential victims include recommendations concerning (a) procedural issues, (b) developing trust and rapport, and (c) specific language and messaging that should be conveyed to these survivors (Macy & Graham, 2012). Regarding language, it was recommended that providers avoid using terms such as "trafficking" and "coercion" and instead use open-ended questions such as "I would be interested to hear…" when asking questions about the individuals' experiences. Additional suggestions were for providers to question potential victims while they are alone (i.e., separated from potential trafficker), focus on their needs and safety, and clearly explain the provider's role and institutions' confidentiality policies (Macy & Graham, 2012). All of this should be done with an emphasis on cultural competence and in the language of the potential survivor.

### *3.2.1 Screening and Identification Tools*

At the time of this publication, no "gold standard" or universally used measures were available for identifying adults or minors who have survived or are currently experiencing sex trafficking. However, over the past two decades, several measures have been developed for use with this population in a variety of settings. Many of these instruments are setting specific (e.g., emergency department, social services) and have undergone only partial or minimal psychometric examination. Furthermore, prior to the development of validated screeners, providers often utilized semi-structured interviews and the clinician's judgment to identify survivors of sex trafficking, so this recent growth in instrument development is significant. Of note, while there are available screening tools that focus on human trafficking more broadly, given the aim of this book, the tools discussed in this chapter are focused on sex trafficking specifically.

#### 3.2.1.1 Screening and Identification Tools for Minors

**The Commercial Sexual Exploitation of Children Screening Tool**
The Commercial Sexual Exploitation of Children (CSEC; CSEC Collaborative Response Team, 2015) screening tool was developed to identify commercial sexual exploitation in 11–18-year-old adolescents. This 22-item tool was developed by the San Luis Obispo County CSEC Collaborative Response Team to determine a minor's level of risk in order to make the appropriate service referrals. The CSEC is not used as an interview tool; instead, it is used by agency personnel when reviewing a child's case information. With total scores ranging from 0 to 54, a higher total score corresponds to a higher degree of risk. While this screening tool is readily available online, psychometric information is not available.

**The Commercial Sexual Exploitation Identification Tool**
Developed by the WestCoast Children's Clinic, the Commercial Sexual Exploitation Identification Tool (CSE-IT; Basson, 2017) was designed to identify individuals aged 10–18 who have experienced current or historic commercial sexual exploitation. Like the CSEC, the CSE-IT was not developed as a self-report questionnaire or as a structured interview, but rather as part of a record review. The CSE-IT has eight key indicators: housing and caregiving, prior abuse or trauma, physical health and appearance, environment and exposure, relationship and personal belongings, signs of current trauma, coercion, and exploitation. Within each key indicator, there are a series of statements to consider and are scored based on "level of concern." Each statement is scored 0–2 (no information, 0; no concern, 0; possible concern, 1; and clear concern, 2). With a maximum total score of 23, a range between 0 and 3 indicates no concern, 4–8 indicates possible concern, and a range of 9–23 indicates that there is a clear concern that the youth has experienced commercial sexual exploitation. The manual encourages providers to collect information from multiple sources and does not rely on the youth as the only point of data collection. Validation studies were conducted across 45 agencies over a period of 15 months. Expert review was used to determine content validity, and concurrent validity (92%) was found to be good. Cronbach's alpha scores for each key indicator range from 0.65 to 0.87. The CSE-IT screening tool and manual are accessible online.

**Greenbaum Six-Item Screening Questionnaire**

There is a large body of evidence indicating that sex trafficking victims, including children and minors, experience many medical conditions as a result of their abuse, and research reveals that these individuals do seek out medical care (Hurst et al., 2021; Beck et al., 2015; Greenbaum et al., 2015). A Six-Item Screening Questionnaire was designed by Greenbaum and their colleagues Greenbaum et al. (2015) to quickly assess high-risk youth ages 12 to 18 years old in a medical setting. Total scores of the six binary "yes" or "no" items range from zero to six, with one point added for each affirmative answer. A cutoff score of two and above is indicative of child sex trafficking and the provider should inquire further. Using the cutoff score of two, the six-item screener demonstrated a sensitivity of 92%, a specificity of 73%, a positive predictive value of 51%, and a negative predictive value of 97%. Other reliability and validity measures were not published. The six items include information on (a) previous history of drug and/or alcohol use; (b) if the youth ever ran away from home; (c) involvement with law enforcement; (d) any history of breaking a bone, traumatic loss of consciousness, or significant wound; (e) history of a sexually transmitted disease; and (f) history of sexual activity with more than five partners. While the questions may be asked directly to the youth, the information may also be gathered from review of medical records.

In 2021, researchers examined the efficacy of Greenbaum Six-Item Screening Questionnaire using a confidential and electronic version in a pediatric emergency room setting (Hurst et al., 2021). They hypothesized that the private nature and technological interface of a confidential electronic screening method would allow providers to obtain more reliable and accurate answers. Using both English and Spanish language versions of the digital questionnaire, minors aged 12–17 completed the six-item screening tool on an electronic tablet while alone, in order to ensure confidentiality. Subjects with a positive screen result, two or more positive "yes" responses, were given four additional questions exploring sex trafficking-specific questions. The digital version of the six-item screener demonstrated a sensitivity of 84.6%, a specificity of 53.2%, a positive predictive value of 20.2%, and a negative predictive value of 96.1%. Reliability statistics were not reported (Hurst et al., 2021). Of the 212 patients analyzed, only 4 surveys were completed in Spanish, and researchers acknowledged that there were likely unknown cultural and linguistic factors that could have decreased the detection of these high-risk youth. This method of digital and confidential screening may be helpful in other busy clinical settings and could decrease the burden of imposed by more time-consuming semi-structured interviews that require in-person screening.

**Greenbaum 17-Item Screening Questionnaire**

A 17-Item Screening Questionnaire (Greenbaum et al., 2018) was created from the original six-item tool and was designed for individuals ranging in age from 13 to 17 years old. Data was collected from 810 minors (male; $n = 121$) located at multiple child advocacy centers, teen clinics, and emergency departments. Nine questions are included in the initial portion of the questionnaire, and the provider is instructed to ask questions 10 through 17 if there is an affirmative response to question nine (Have you ever had sex of any type?). The 17-item screener demonstrated a sensitivity of 84.4%, specificity of 57.5%, positive predictive value of 19.9%, and a negative predictive value 96.7%. The full screener is available as supplemental material with the primary validation publication and includes instructions for introducing the questionnaire to the minor. Additionally, a supplemental set of questions is also available for medical professionals. One critique of similar screeners with binary responses is that they are unable to measure frequency and severity, which could be important information when determining next steps (Romero et al., 2021).

The limited availability of validated identification tools is evident in a recent systematic review of available assessment tools that were specifically designed to screen or identify sex-trafficked minors (Romero et al., 2021). Following a thorough search of reputable online academic databases and subsequent exclusion of inappropriate articles, only one screening instrument was identified (17-Item Screening Questionnaire; Greenbaum et al., 2018). When determining whether an instrument was appropriate for review, articles were removed if they were (a) not in English, (b) not based in the United States, (c) not specific to child sex trafficking, and (d) did not use a structured format for screening/identification. After the authors expanded their search to Google, a total of four instruments were identified as appropriate for review, all of which were included in this chapter above (Table 3.1).

#### 3.2.1.2 Screening and Identification Tools for Adults

**The Trafficking Victim Identification Tool**

The Trafficking Victim Identification Tool (TVIT; Table 3.2) is a structured interview developed by the Vera Institute of Justice and includes a domain specific to sexual exploitation (Simich et al., 2014). The five domains were revealed by factor analysis, and the four other domains are (a) force, fraud, and coercion, (b) isolation, (c) labor, and (d) harm. TVIT was designed as a comprehensive assessment tool for social services settings. Two versions are available including short (20 items) and long (53 items) forms which are easily accessible online and include a full manual. While the TVIT can be used as a screening tool, the long version can take over 40 minutes and may be more effective during an in-depth assessment rather than a brief screening process. All items rely on the individual's self-report and use a mixture of open- and close-ended questions. The TVIT was validated across a variety of clinical and forensic settings. Psychometric properties of the long version indicate an inter-rater reliability using Cohen's K of 0.89, Cronbach's alpha of 0.91, and good criterion validity using Cohen's K (Simich et al., 2014). While shorter versions of the tool demonstrated good psychometric evidence, the long version consistently outperformed the other versions. The TVIT takes culture into consideration, including questions about the individual's English language proficiency prior to conducting the interview as well as the use of an interpreter. Additionally, the TVIT includes migration-specific questions for individuals that are foreign-born. While the TVIT was validated with a small sample of minors, critiques suggest that

**Table 3.1** Child/minor sex trafficking identification tools and psychometric evidence

| Measure | First author and year | Scale format | Reliability | Validity |
|---|---|---|---|---|
| Commercial Sexual Exploitation of Children (CSEC) screening tool | CSEC Collaborative Response Team (2015) | "Yes," "no," or "unknown" answers, checklist of indicators | N/A | N/A |
| Commercial Sexual Exploitation Identification Tool (CSE-IT) | Basson (2017) | Information collected is scored on a 3-point scale (0 = no concern to 2 = clear concern), eight domains | Cronbach's alpha of 0.65 to 0.87 | Expert review to determine content validity<br>Concurrent validity (92%) |
| Greenbaum Six-Item Screening Questionnaire | Greenbaum et al. (2015) | Dichotomous "Yes" or "No," six items with a cutoff of two positive answers | N/A | Sensitivity (92%)<br>Specificity (73%)<br>Positive predictive value (51%)<br>Negative predictive value (97%) |
| Greenbaum Six-Item Screening Questionnaire (confidential electronic version) | Hurst et al. (2021) | Dichotomous "Yes" or "No," six items with a cutoff of two positive answers | N/A | Sensitivity (84.6%)<br>Specificity (53.2%)<br>Positive predictive value (20.2%)<br>Negative predictive value (96.1%) |
| Greenbaum 17-Item Screening Questionnaire | Greenbaum et al. (2018) | 17 Dichotomous "Yes" or "No" items | N/A | Sensitivity (84.4%)<br>Specificity (57.5%)<br>Positive predictive value (19.9%)<br>Negative predictive value (96.7%) |

modifications should be made to the language and questions if it were to be used to identify commercial sexual exploitation of minors (US Department of Justice, 2016). One weakness identified by the authors of the TVIT is that it does not collect information about sexual orientation, which may be significant for identifying minors involved in sex trafficking (Simich et al., 2014).

**Table 3.2** Adult sex trafficking identification tools and psychometric evidence

| Measure | First author and year | Scale format | Reliability | Validity |
|---|---|---|---|---|
| Rapid Appraisal for Trafficking (RAFT) | Chisolm-Straker et al. (2021) | Four Dichotomous "Yes" or "No" questions from the TVIT | N/A | Sensitivity (92%) Specificity (72%) |
| Mumma 14-question screening survey | Mumma et al. (2017) | 14 Dichotomous "Yes" or "No" items | N/A | Sensitivity (100%), better than physician concern Specificity (78%), below physician concern |
| Trafficking Victim Identification Tool (TVIT) | Simich et al. (2014) | Dichotomous "Yes" or "No," long version 53 items, short version 20 items | Inter-rater reliability Cohen's K of 0.89 Cronbach's alpha of 0.91 | Good criterion validity using Cohen's K |

**The Rapid Appraisal for Trafficking**

Aiming to develop a tool to quickly screen for adult trafficking victims in an emergency department setting, researchers used the TVIT as the reference standard when constructing the Rapid Appraisal for Trafficking (RAFT; Chisolm-Straker et al., 2021). The four dichotomous TVIT questions that were included in the RAFT were chosen as they had the highest odds of predicting trafficking. The questionnaire items are as follows: Have you ever (a) worked, or done other things, in a place that made you feel scared or unsafe? (b) Have you been tricked or forced into doing any kind of work that you did not want to do? (c) Have you been afraid to leave or quit a work situation due to fears of violence or threats of harm to yourself or your family? (d) Have you received anything in exchange for sex? The RAFT was designed to identify both sex- and labor-trafficked individuals so not to under detect one of the two groups. Affirmative responses to at least one item demonstrated a sensitivity of 92% and specificity of 72%. The authors suggest that once identified, these trafficked individuals should be provided with an opportunity to speak with a social worker, receive medical care specific to their trafficking experiences, and make a report to law enforcement or the National Human Trafficking Hotline (Chisolm-Straker et al., 2021). It was also suggested that each emergency department utilizing the RAFT develops site-specific protocols of where to privately triage patients and identifies who conducts the triage and the steps that should follow a positive screening.

**Mumma 14-Question Survey**

Given the high number of survivors of sex trafficking that seek medical care, a 14-question survey was designed to screen specifically for sex trafficking in an emergency room setting (Mumma et al., 2017). Administered to medically stable female patients between the ages of 18 and 40, the 14-question survey was intended to be administered in less than 10 minutes. Answering "yes" to any of the screening questions was defined as a "a positive survey screening." Following the completion of the survey, the physician that administered the survey indicates whether they were concerned that the patient may be a victim of sex trafficking. Results of the pilot study demonstrated the 100% sensitivity and 78% specificity. While the sensitivity of the survey was better than physician concern, specificity of the instrument was below physician concern. All "true positives," individuals who acknowledged being a victim of sex trafficking, answered "yes" to question two ("Were you (or anyone you work with) ever beaten, hit, yelled at, raped, threatened, or made to feel physical pain for working slowly or for trying to leave?"). Since the results of this measure required women to acknowledge their involvement in sex trafficking, one weakness of the 14-question survey was the possibility of false negatives as some survivors of sex trafficking may not acknowledge involvement.

### 3.2.2 *Response Following Identification*

Once the screening tool is completed and the individual is identified as a survivor of sex trafficking, an immediate response may be needed by the provider. If the identified survivor of sex trafficking is under the age of 18, the providers are obligated to notify the appropriate authorities according to local reporting laws. Throughout the literature, it is often suggested that service providers immediately contact the National Human Trafficking Resource Center's hotline (1-888-373-7888) to help aid the identified individual and seek further information (Chisolm-Straker et al., 2021). Additional recommendations, especially for adult survivors, include engaging the individual in a discussion around the decision to contact authorities prior to making the call, thoroughly assessing the individual's imminent level of risk of harm to themselves and others, and developing a safety plan (Chisolm-Straker et al., 2021; Macy & Graham, 2012).

## 3.3 Assessing Symptoms, Needs, and Outcomes

Individuals who have survived sex trafficking present with a sequela of symptoms as well as specific needs that are wide-ranging. Primary categories include substance use disorders (Cyders et al., 2021; Levine, 2017), anxiety and depressive disorders (Hopper & Gonzalez, 2018; Levine, 2017), posttraumatic stress and other trauma-related disorders (Hopper & Gonzalez, 2018; Le et al., 2018; Levine, 2017), reproductive and other health issues (Bauer et al., 2019; Le et al., 2018; Lederer & Wetzel, 2014), and chronic pain (Levine, 2017; Farley et al., 2016).

Similar to screening and identification tools, there are no "gold standard" measures for assessing symptoms, needs, or outcomes for those who have survived sex

trafficking. Graham et al. (2019) conducted a systematic review and identified measures that were used to gather data on the needs and service outcomes of individuals who have experienced sex trafficking. With a review spanning articles published between 2002 and 2017, the authors found that of the 53 studies identified, most acknowledged that the measures used during data collection were not developed or validated with individuals who survived sex trafficking (Graham et al., 2019).

Given the high rates of posttraumatic stress and other trauma-related disorders within the sex-trafficked population, a trauma-informed approach during the psychological assessment of trafficked persons is warranted (Hopper, 2017). The assessment process should initially focus on rapport-building and assessing the individuals' immediate safety and needs, as more complex emotional difficulties cannot be addressed when there is imminent risk. Trauma-informed feedback and psychoeducation during the assessment process normalize the individual's experiences, creating a better understanding as to the reasons they are experiencing specific symptoms. It is recommended that the assessment is concluded with a focus on strengths, coping strategies, and goals for the future, in order to create the first steps toward a healing process (Hopper, 2017). A trauma-informed lens allows clinicians to assess the individual within the context of their lived experiences, and when adequate compassion is demonstrated during that process, the quality of the information collected is improved (Goldenson et al., 2022; Hopper, 2017).

Gathering information on the lived experiences of these individuals should not be limited to one survivor's assessment but rather included in the larger anti-trafficking efforts. The inclusion of survivors in anti-trafficking efforts should also incorporate the perspectives of survivors during the development and validation of assessment measures (Lockyer, 2020). Powers and Paul (2018) highlight this need:

> Without survivor input we can't know if our outreach and awareness campaigns meant to reach victims are going to be effective. We can't know if our shelters and direct service programmes will uphold the standards of excellence achieved through culturally competent, trauma-informed care. We can't know if our efforts to identify victims will reach those most entrenched and isolated.

Survivors' perspectives should inform research and the development of assessment measures to ensure that their needs are appropriately represented and identified (Lockyer, 2020; Barnert et al., 2017).

## 3.4 Considerations and Recommendations

The past decade has produced a significant increase in the number of screeners designed to identify individuals who are experiencing or have survived sex trafficking. While researchers often examine aspects of the screening tool validity, rigorous review of reliability is often overlooked. Further psychometric investigation of the sex trafficking screening and identification tools discussed in this chapter could serve as an important next step. Additionally, an examination of available literature reveals a dearth of validated assessments that are designed to measure the symptoms and needs of individuals who have survived sex trafficking. Without rigorous measurement standards and the thorough examination of psychometric properties, it will remain unclear how effective the available tools are at measuring the factors that providers believe they are measuring in these individuals.

Considering the populations that are impacted by sex trafficking (discussed in Chap. 1), these measures should be examined to test their effectiveness with wide-ranging and diverse populations. The development and validation of these screening and assessment tools should be grounded in survivor-centered and trauma-informed principles with the input of survivors' perspective. Furthermore, making these measures easily accessible, brief, and validated in multiple languages is a necessary step during the development process.

## References

Barnert, E., Iqbal, Z., Bruce, J., Anoshiravani, A., Kolhatkar, G., & Greenbaum, J. (2017). Commercial sexual exploitation and sex trafficking of children and adolescents: A narrative review. *Academic Pediatrics, 17*(8), 825–829.

Barnert, E., Kelly, M., Godoy, S., Abrams, L. S., Rasch, M., et al. (2019). Understanding commercially sexually exploited young women's access to, utilization of, and engagement in health care: "Work around what I need". *Women's Health Issues, 29*(4), 315–324.

Basson, D. (2017). Validation of the commercial sexual exploitation-identification tool (CSE-IT). *Technical report*. WestCoast Children's Clinic.

Bauer, R., Brown, S., Cannon, E., & Southard, E. (2019). What health providers should know about human sex trafficking. *Medsurg Nursing, 28*(6), 347–351.

Beck, M. E., Lineer, M. M., Melzer-Lange, M., Simpson, P., Nugent, M., & Rabbitt, A. (2015). Medical providers' understanding of sex trafficking and their experience with at-risk patients. *Pediatrics, 135*(4), e895–e902. https://doi.org/10.1542/peds.2014-2814

Browne-James, L., Litam, S. D. A., & McRae, L. (2021). Child sex trafficking: Strategies for identification, counseling, and advocacy. *International Journal for the Advancement of Counselling, 43*(2), 113–123.

Chisolm-Straker, M., Singer, E., Strong, D., Loo, G. T., Rothman, E. F., Clesca, C., … Richardson, L. D. (2021). Validation of a screening tool for labor and sex trafficking among emergency department patients. *Journal of the American College of Emergency Physicians Open, 2*(5), e12558.

Chisolm-Straker, M., Sze, J., Einbond, J., White, J., & Stoklosa, H. (2019). Screening for human trafficking among homeless young adults. *Children and Youth Services Review, 98*, 72–79.

CSEC Collaborative Response Team. (2015). *Commercially sexually exploited children (CSEC): Screening tool*. Retrieved from https://www.cwda.org/sites/main/files/file-attachments/slo-csecscreening-tool-3-5-15.pdf

Cyders, M. A., Hunton, T., & Hershberger, A. R. (2021). Substance use and childhood sexual abuse among girls who are victims of commercial sexual exploitation. *Substance Use & Misuse, 56*(9), 1339–1345.

Farley, M., Deer, S., Golding, J. M., Matthews, N., Lopez, G., Stark, C., & Hudon, E. (2016). The prostitution and trafficking of American Indian/Alaska Native women in Minnesota. *American Indian and Alaska Native Mental Health Research, 23*(1), 65–104.

Franklin, C. A., & Menaker, T. A. (2015, April). The impact of observer characteristics on blame assessments of prostituted female youth. *Feminist Criminology, 10*(2), 140–164.

Goldenson, J., Brodsky, S. L., & Perlin, M. L. (2022). Trauma-informed forensic mental health assessment: Practical implications, ethical tensions, and alignment with therapeutic jurisprudence principles. *Psychology, Public Policy, and Law.*, *28*(2), 226–239.

Graham, L. M., Macy, R. J., Eckhardt, A., Rizo, C. F., & Jordan, B. L. (2019). Measures for evaluating sex trafficking aftercare and support services: A systematic review and resource compilation. *Aggression and Violent Behavior, 47*, 117–136.

Greenbaum, V. J., Dodd, M., & McCracken, C. (2015). A short screening tool to identify victims of child sex trafficking in the health care setting. *Pediatric Emergency Care, 34*(1), 33–37. https://doi.org/10.1097/PEC.0000000000000602

Greenbaum, V. J., Livings, M. S., Lai, B. S., Edinburgh, L., Baikie, P., Grant, S. R., … Self-Brown, S. (2018). Evaluation of a tool to identify child sex trafficking victims in multiple healthcare settings. *Journal of Adolescent Health, 63*(6), 745–752. https://doi.org/10.1016/j.jadohealth.2018.06.032

Haney, K., LeBeau, K., Bodner, S., Czizik, A., Young, M. E., et al. (2020). Sex trafficking in the United States: A scoping review. *Journal of Evidence-Based Social Work, 17*(6), 714–748.

Hopper, E. K. (2017). Trauma-informed psychological assessment of human trafficking survivors. *Women & Therapy, 40*(1–2), 12–30.

Hopper, E. K., & Gonzalez, L. D. (2018). A comparison of psychological symptoms in survivors of sex and labor trafficking. *Behavioral Medicine, 44*(3), 177–188. https://doi.org/10.1080/08964289.2018.1432551

Hurst, I. A., Abdoo, D. C., Harpin, S., Leonard, J., & Adelgais, K. (2021). Confidential screening for sex trafficking among minors in a pediatric emergency department. *Pediatrics, 147*(3). https://doi.org/10.1542/peds.2020-013235

Kennedy, M. A., Arebalos, M. R., Ekroos, R. A., & Cimino, A. N. (2021). Sex trafficking red flags: Confirming presentation patterns and childhood adversity risk factors. *Nurse Leader, 19*(5), 516–520.

Le, P. D., Ryan, N., Rosenstock, Y., & Goldmann, E. (2018). Health issues associated with commercial sexual exploitation and sex trafficking of children in the United States: A systematic review. *Behavioral Medicine, 44*(3), 219–233.

Lederer, L. J., & Wetzel, C. A. (2014). The health consequences of sex trafficking and their implications for identifying victims in healthcare facilities. *Annals of Health Law, 23*, 61.

Levine, J. A. (2017). Mental health issues in survivors of sex trafficking. *Cogent Medicine, 4*(1), 1278841.

Lockyer, S. (2020). Beyond inclusion: Survivor-leader voice in anti-human trafficking organizations. *Journal of Human Trafficking*, 1–22. https://doi.org/10.1080/23322705.2020.1756122

Macy, R. J., & Graham, L. M. (2012). Identifying domestic and international sex-trafficking victims during human service provision. *Trauma, Violence, & Abuse, 13*(2), 59–76.

Marcinkowski, B., Caggiula, A., Tran, B. N., Tran, Q. K., & Pourmand, A. (2022). Sex trafficking screening and intervention in the emergency department: A scoping review. *Journal of the American College of Emergency Physicians Open, 3*(1), e12638.

Mumma, B. E., Scofield, M. E., Mendoza, L. P., Toofan, Y., Youngyunpipatkul, J., & Hernandez, B. (2017). Screening for victims of sex trafficking in the emergency department: A pilot program. *Western Journal of Emergency Medicine, 18*(4), 616.

Powers, L., & Paul, N. (2018). *The need for survivor-informed research to fight human trafficking*. https://delta87.org/2018/11/need-survivor-informed-research-fight human trafficking/?fbclid=IwAR3pVFWNBxWtRbNEBTx4u0Vwuk8_2i2GFBE1kNUodFfFXfz5a3TgU3xbOco

Rafferty, Y. (2016). Challenges to the rapid identification of children who have been trafficked for commercial sexual exploitation. *Child Abuse & Neglect, 52*, 158–168.

Rajaram, S. S., & Tidball, S. (2018). Survivors' voices – Complex needs of sex trafficking survivors in the Midwest. *Behavioral Medicine, 44*(3), 189–198.

Reid, J. A., & Jones, S. (2011). Exploited vulnerability: Legal and psychological perspectives on child sex trafficking victims. *Victims and Offenders, 6*(2), 207–231.

Romero, D. E., Interiano-Shiverdecker, C. G., Castellon, N. E., & Strentzsch, J. (2021). A review of child sex trafficking instruments. *Journal of child and adolescent counseling, 7*(1), 56–69.

Simich, L., Goyen, L., Powell, A., & Mallozzi, K. (2014). *Improving human trafficking victim identification: Validation and dissemination of a screening tool*. Vera Institute of Justice. https://www.vera.org/downloads/publications/human-trafficking-identification-tool-technical-report.pdf

U.S. Department of Health and Human Services. (2008). *Resources: Identifying and interacting with victims of human trafficking*. Author. https://www.acf.hhs.gov/sites/default/files/documents/orr/tips_for_identifying_and_helping_victims_of_human_trafficking.pdf

U.S. Department of Justice. (2016). *Memorandum summarizing the available screening tools to identify Commercially Sexually Exploited Children (CSEC)*. https://nicic.gov/memorandum-summarizing-available-screening-tools-identify-commercially-sexually-exploited-children

Wiener, R. L., Berry, M. C., Wertheimer, J., Petty, T., & Martinez, J. (2021, May). The public's judgement of sex trafficked women: Blaming the victim? *Journal of Experimental Psychology: Applied, 27*(3), 529–545.

# Chapter 4
# Theories and Conceptual Models

**Abstract** This chapter describes relevant theories and proposed models for understanding the nature of traumatization that results from the experience of sex trafficking, including a focus on trauma and gender violence. The discussion focuses on complex posttraumatic stress disorder (cPTSD), sociocultural theories of traumatization, and the relevance of intimate partner violence (IPV) and the battered woman syndrome (BWS) to understanding the experience of sex trafficking survivors.

**Keywords** Sex trafficking · Victim · Survivor · Traumatization · cPTSD · Complex posttraumatic stress disorder

## 4.1 Introduction

There is no consensus or single unifying theory that describes the experience of the sex trafficking survivor. There is a great deal of variability among survivors, including developmental background (including whether it was optimal or characterized by adverse experiences), circumstances under which they were trafficked, and complexity of the issue of consent and its relevance to the experience of the survivor. Choice is, by definition, often limited for someone who is being trafficked; however, some survivors have even less choice, for example, over who the clients or buyers are, what types of services are offered, and whether condoms are used (Meshkovska et al., 2015). The less choice a trafficked person has, the higher the likelihood that the experience will be traumatizing and that the survivor will be at higher risk for various adverse outcomes associated with traumatization.

All of that said, there are some existing theories, conceptual frameworks, or psychological constructs that can usefully inform our understanding of the experience of the trafficking survivor by virtue of their discussion of captivity and complex traumatization. These include Judith Herman's elucidation of complex posttraumatic stress disorder (cPTSD), Lenore Walker's contributions to understanding intimate partner violence (IPV) and the battered woman syndrome, feminist theory, and intersectional and critical race theory (CRT) perspectives. In addition,

 
J. Davidtz et al., *Sex Trafficking*, SpringerBriefs in Psychology,
https://doi.org/10.1007/978-3-031-09120-9_4

socioeconomic theory and ecological systems theory contribute to an understanding of the persistence of the industry of sex trafficking. Though the latter are important to consider in order to understand and effect change within the landscape of this major public health problem and its sequelae, they are beyond the scope of the current chapter, which is focused more on the survivor experience and practice recommendations for treating survivors of CSE.

## 4.2 Risk Factors and Phenomenology

Before elaborating upon theories that inform the survivor's experience and treatment, it is important to acknowledge some of the characteristics that make people vulnerable to trafficking and the relevance of those features to the sequelae, outcomes, and phenomenology of the post-trafficking survivor experience.

Studies on sex trafficking consistently highlight the finding that most survivors of trafficking come from backgrounds and environments characterized by systematic disadvantage and a host of other traumatic and adverse experiences, including individual factors like sexual, physical, or emotional abuse, poverty, homelessness, minority status, or growing up in a high crime neighborhood; psychosocial factors like immigration, language barriers, and legal or child welfare system involvement; and systemic factors, like political instability, discrimination, racism, and gender-based inequalities (Contreras et al., 2017; Hopper & Gonzalez, 2018; Salami et al., 2018). These factors make the person more vulnerable to being trafficked and to the effects of the trafficker's coercive control of them (Hopper & Gonzalez, 2018; Kim, 2011, in Contreras et al., 2017). Furthermore, people who have experienced some form of trauma prior to being trafficked may be less resilient to the trauma of being trafficked and may be at especially high risk for more severe symptoms, including dissociation, and greater functional impairment (Cole et al., 2016).

The sequelae of sex trafficking are multifold and wide-ranging. Survivors experience enduring physical and psychological/emotional symptoms (Meshkovska et al., 2015), as well as practical challenges and obstacles that hinder the process of recovery and reintegration, and social and occupational functioning. For example, Goldberg and Moore (2018) describe a range of adverse outcomes experienced by CSE survivors, including physical injuries; infections like STIs and pelvic inflammatory disease; gynecological issues associated with pregnancy, abortion, and sexual trauma; malnourishment; and poor dental hygiene. In a systematic review of health problems associated with trafficking, Ottisova et al. (2016) found that people who are trafficked report having experienced high levels of violence and endorse an array of physical complaints, including headaches, stomach pain, and back pain. Furthermore, in one study by Hossain et al. (2010), injuries and sexual violence experienced during trafficking were found to be associated with higher levels of posttraumatic symptoms, depression, and anxiety.

Survivors present with a range of significant psychiatric issues, suicidal ideation and behavior, and nonsuicidal self-injurious behavior (NSSI; Goldberg & Moore,

2018). The most frequently documented psychological symptoms reported by, and observed in, survivors of commercial sexual exploitation include complex trauma, PTSD, dissociation, suicidality, anxiety and depression, and substance abuse (Cecchet & Thoburn, 2014; Cole et al., 2016; Lanctot et al., 2020; Oram et al., 2015; Ottisova et al., 2016). Survivors also experience disruptions in their identity or sense of self and their capacity to relate to others and maintain appropriate interpersonal boundaries (Cole et al., 2016; Contreras et al., 2017). Hopper and Gonzalez (2018) note that, although there are few studies that have directly investigated complex trauma in trafficking survivors, symptoms of complex PTSD, including emotional and behavioral dysregulation, are commonly endorsed by survivors of CSE. Severe emotional and behavioral dysregulation and disruption of normal developmental processes cause significant functional and relational impairment and present challenges for providers, including therapists (Cole et al., 2016).

In addition to coping with debilitating emotional/psychiatric symptoms, some survivors must contend with the challenges of trying to live and function independently when they have never had the opportunity to acquire basic skills of living. This may be especially true for survivors who were trafficked when they were minors or experienced neglect and abuse in their families of origin (Gold, 2000).

What follows is a brief summary of theories or conceptual models that shed some light on the trafficking experience and the implications for treatment. Given the high rates of childhood abuse and other earlier traumas (Contreras et al., 2017; Hopper & Gonzalez, 2018) among people who have been trafficked and the nature of being trafficked as a form of captivity, Judith Herman's elucidation of cPTSD and the three-phase treatment she recommends are especially salient. Indeed, Herman's theory was informed, in part, by her work with survivors of various types of torture and captivity, including human trafficking. Similarly, Lenore Walker's description of the cycle of intimate partner violence and battered woman syndrome closely parallels the nature of the relationship between trafficker and victim and provides a context within which to understand some of the relational complexities of abusive relationships and why it is so difficult for victims to extricate themselves from those relationships. Finally, an understanding of the problem of sex trafficking and its sequelae would be incomplete without acknowledging the sociopolitical context within which it occurs. Thus, we integrate contributions from feminist theory, intersectionality, and critical race theory as they relate to IPV and the ongoing problem of commercial sexual exploitation, particularly of women.

## 4.3 Complex PTSD: A Model for Understanding the Effects of Captivity and Coercive Control

Judith Herman first described the unique sequelae of prolonged and repeated trauma and proposed the diagnosis of complex posttraumatic stress disorder (cPTSD) in 1992 (Herman, 1992a, b). Since then, empirical and clinical data continue to demonstrate it to be a clinically relevant elucidation of a syndrome experienced by survivors of repeated, prolonged trauma that is distinct from, though often comorbid with, PTSD (Ford & Courtois, 2009). cPTSD has since been included in the ICD-11 and, though it is not in the DSM-5, the DSM-5 PTSD criteria were updated to include a specifier for dissociation and a domain for affective changes, which are highly characteristic of cPTSD but, prior to DSM-5, had not been included in the diagnostic criteria for PTSD.

One of the most notable contributions of this clinical entity and its features is the explication of the ways in which captivity, coercive control, and cruelty within the interpersonal context not only cause severe posttraumatic symptoms, but also are damaging to the person's identity, relationships, and capacity for emotion regulation. This is highly relevant to the experience of sex trafficking, given the complexity of survivors' relationships with their abusers, and the inherent ambivalence they experience within those relationships.

In addition to often experiencing typical symptoms of PTSD, depression, and anxiety, people who have experienced repeated, prolonged victimization and the systems of coercive control within which that victimization takes place (Contreras et al., 2017; Herman, 1992a, b; Herman, 2003) show disturbances in three other broad areas of functioning: they have complex, multiproblem, and chronic symptom presentations, they experience significant changes in identity or personality or what Herman (1992a, b) calls "deformations" of relatedness and identity, and they are vulnerable to being revictimized or to various forms of self-harm.

### 4.3.1 Symptomatic Features

People who are chronically abused and traumatized experience a wider range and greater severity of psychiatric symptoms and are more likely to present with multiple comorbidities (Herman, 1992a, b; Ford & Courtois, 2009). In addition to symptoms like flashbacks, nightmares, and insomnia, they suffer persistent and severe hyperarousal of the nervous system. They also tend to suffer associated somatic complaints, like chronic back and pelvic pain, tension headaches, and gastrointestinal problems. They are prone to severe dissociative experiences that can take various forms, including depersonalization, derealization, and fragmentation. In the affective domain, survivors of CSE suffer severe and intractable depression (Cole et al., 2016). Herman (1992a, b) posits that the severe depression experienced by survivors of prolonged trauma is, in part, a manifestation of unexpressed anger and rage at their perpetrators and others who were complicit and did not protect or help them. She also notes that "internalization of rage may result in a malignant self-hatred and chronic suicidality" (Herman, 1992a, b; p. 382).

### 4.3.2 Characterological Features

In addition to the symptomatic sequelae, the coercive control that characterizes prolonged victimization produces characterological changes in the form of pathological changes in identity and the capacity for relatedness (Ford & Courtois, 2009; Herman, 1992a, b).

"While the victim of a single acute trauma may say she is 'not herself' since the event, the victim of chronic trauma might lose the sense that she has a self" (Herman, 1992a, b; p. 385). The disturbances in identity that result from chronic traumatization manifest in various ways, including a pervasive experience of shame and a sense of the self as defective, contaminated, or bad; an absence of an integrated sense of the self across time and situations, splitting-based views of the self and others as is seen in borderline personality disorder (Kernberg, 1984) in (Herman, 1992a, b); and a fragmentation of the self, which, at its most severe, can manifest as dissociated self-states such as are observed in dissociative identity disorder (Chefetz, 2015; Herman, 1992a, b; Howell, 2011; Putnam, 1989, 2016).

Prolonged victimization and psychological coercion profoundly undermine the quality of the person's relationships with others. Being in captivity under coercive control results in the perpetrator becoming the most influential and powerful person in a victim's life and their actions and beliefs shaping the victim's psychology (Contreras et al., 2017; Herman, 1992a, b; Herman, 2003). Coercive control is established via strategies that are "designed to instill terror and helplessness, to destroy the victim's sense of self in relation to others, and to foster a pathologic attachment to the perpetrator" (Herman, 1992a, b; p. 383). These strategies include the threat of violence, humiliation, and controlling bodily functions or depriving the victim of basic needs until their autonomy is destroyed, and they are under the complete control of the perpetrator. Abusers also isolate their victims from other people so that they become completely dependent on them for both basic and emotional needs and, perhaps most destructively, abusers force their victims to witness or participate in crimes against others (Contreras et al., 2017; Herman, 1992a, b).

The result of isolating the victim and making them completely dependent on the perpetrator is a phenomenon whereby the victim comes to identify with their captor or abuser known as "traumatic bonding." This bond, along with the diminished sense of autonomy that results from being controlled by, and entirely dependent upon, the perpetrator, makes it difficult for victims to leave even if they have opportunities to do so (Herman, 1992a, b). This has been described as a central mechanism in the experience of battered women (Walker, 2016) and is relevant to survivors of CSE as well. Indeed, in the case of sex trafficking, it may be one reason some survivors do not think of themselves as victims who have been trafficked, which is one of the major barriers to reintegrating and accessing treatment and other resources (Contreras et al., 2017).

The relational sequelae of traumatic bonding persist even after escape, serving as a template for the survivor's other relationships and, in some cases, keeping the perpetrator alive in the internal world of the survivor. As a result, survivors approach the world and relationships with distrust and bewilderment. Because their abusers were sources of both cruelty and comfort, they are prone to relating in extremes and may vacillate between enmeshed attachment, on the one hand, and frightened withdrawal, on the other hand (Herman, 1992a, b). This type of relational pathology may be especially pronounced in people who were abused and/or trafficked as children, given their experience of earlier disruptions in attachment. As a result, they may present with a pattern of relating that is characterized by intense vacillation between idealization and devaluation or closeness and distance, as seen in borderline personality disorder (Herman, 1992a, b; Kernberg, 1984).

### 4.3.3 *Vulnerability to Repeated Harm*

Survivors of captivity and prolonged victimization are at increased risk for repeated victimization. This may take the form of vulnerability to being victimized by others or persistent self-inflicted harm in the form of nonsuicidal self-injurious behavior (van der Kolk, 1992 in Herman, 1992a, b). For trafficking survivors, this may happen by way of a return to their trafficker or pimp, and addressing and mitigating the risk of this are important considerations in treatment.

One of the most notable contributions of Herman's observations is the value they have for reducing stigmatization of chronically traumatized people. Though the presenting features of personality pathology and chronic traumatization may be similar, understanding the ways in which their core underlying structures are distinct has implications for access to, and the experience of, appropriate care. This conceptualization is especially relevant to the experience of survivors of trafficking, given that they are often stigmatized, blamed, and even prosecuted, for their victimization.

## 4.4 Sex Trafficking, Intimate Partner Violence, and Feminist Theory

Although there is no single profile of a survivor of sex trafficking, available data suggest that females are disproportionately vulnerable to sex trafficking (Polaris, 2021). Individuals who have survived sex trafficking and those who have survived intimate partner violence (IPV) are more similar than different in their experiences of abuse, trauma, and victimization (Roe-Sepowitz et al., 2014). Overlapping characteristics and experiences include violence and trauma, subjection to dominance and power, psychological abuse and instability, economic control, as well as challenges related to disclosure and escape. Furthermore, examination of available data suggests that over one-third of survivors of sex trafficking, whose recruitment method was known, were recruited by an intimate partner or proposition of marriage (Polaris, 2021). Researchers examining demographic trends of sex trafficking in Midwestern regions of the United States found that sex trafficking was most frequently experienced within the contexts of a romantic relationship, which made up 28% of the known sample (Nichols et al., 2022).

Feminist theory is perhaps the most instrumental theoretical framework in forming the current understanding of violence against women. The feminist framework is a "broad, transdisciplinary perspective that strives to understand roles, experiences, and values of individuals on the basis of gender" (Gerassi, 2015; p. 2). From examination of IPV relationships and echoed in sex trafficking research, feminist theorists have put forth many theoretical concepts to better understand these relationships and victimizations. While not an exhaustive list, these concepts include the battered woman syndrome, learned helplessness, the cycle of violence, aspects of power and control, the relationship patriarchy and other systemic influences, and intersectionality (McLeod et al., 2020; Walker, 2016; Gerassi, 2015). Parallel to IPV, associations between those who are trafficked and their traffickers are characterized by an unequal power dynamic. This unequal dynamic is often maintained by a cycle of violence that was initially identified while examining the phases of abuse and violence that occurred in domestic violence relationships (Walker, 1979).

## 4.5 Learned Helplessness and the Cycle of Violence

Seligman & Beagley (1975) posited that learned helplessness is a psychological phenomenon that results from repeated exposures to uncontrollable and unpleasant events. First observed in laboratory animals, learned helplessness is a behavioral response that arises when an individual experiences continual painful or aversive stimuli that they are unable to escape. In time, the individual stops trying to avoid the situation or escape altogether. The theory of learned helplessness has been used to examine the experiences of both survivors of IPV and sex trafficking, including their apprehension to leave the abusive situation (Hopper & Hidalgo, 2006; Walker, 2016). Increases in violence in a relationship result in an increase in the learned helplessness response in the survivor (Walker, 1984; Wilson et al., 1993).

Informed by the theory of learned helplessness, the cycle of violence is a model that was developed to better understand and describe abusive relationships. There are three distinct phases that have been identified in this model, which is predicated on a tension reduction theory (Walker, 2016). First, there is a tension-building phase that is coupled with increasing feelings of danger. During this phase, the aggressor expresses lower levels of dissatisfaction and hostility, and the woman attempts to mollify the aggressor to keep them from further escalation and aggression (Falcke et al., 2017; Walker, 2016). These attempts to pacify the aggressor often work for a period of time, which reinforces the belief that the survivor is able to control the situation and has a direct influence on the learned helplessness response. As the tension continues to escalate, there comes a time where the survivor is no longer able to appease the aggressor, and the next phase of the cycle – an acute battering incident – begins. As described in Walker's original text, "phase two is characterized by the uncontrollable discharge of the tensions that have built up during phase one" (Walker, 1979, p. 59). This second phase is often when the most severe physical injuries are caused. The eventual end of this phase is reinforcing in and of itself in that that there is a physiological reduction in tension and that the violence has succeeded in achieving the aggressor's goal (Walker, 2016). Moreover, the experience of learned helplessness is intensified as the abuse occurs sporadically, capriciously, and in a way that the victim is unable to prevent, further enhancing the feeling that they are unable to avoid the violence. In phase three, also known as the loving contrition phase, the aggressor often apologizes and expresses kindness or remorse. However, this phase can also be a mere absence of violence or tension without loving-contrition behaviors, or the danger or potential for violence may remain high and never return to a baseline level.

In sex trafficking situations, as with IPV relationships, the initial stages often encompass a period of time without physical aggression where the trafficker appears trustworthy, a concept that is often referred to as grooming (Falcke et al., 2017; Roe-Sepowitz et al., 2014). Occurring over extended time periods, during these relationship beginnings, the victim is conditioned to receive the abuse and not to tell, believing that if they do tell (or leave), they will be blamed or not believed. Furthermore, power and control are strategic tools used to keep survivors of sex trafficking in that situation (Roe-Sepowitz et al., 2014), and the imbalance of power is a key variable that leads to the exertion of coercive control by the trafficker. This power is often extended in control over the survivors' appearance, what they can wear, how they can act, access to money, where they can go and with whom, and the withholding of identifying documents (Litam, 2017).

A notable point of ongoing disagreement between classical feminist theorists is the voluntary nature of any form of sex work. While the neo-abolitionist perspective is that all forms of sex work, voluntary or involuntary, are oppressive against women, the pro-sex work perspective is that there are circumstances where women have the independent choice of sex work (Gerassi, 2015). However, when examining feminist literature, theorists and researchers noted a dearth in the acknowledgment and understanding of the differences of sex trafficking and other forms of violence against women depending on the individual's race and other aspects of identity.

## 4.6 Intersectionality and Critical Race Theory

Kimberle Crenshaw (1991) drew much needed attention to violence against women of color as a consequence of interconnecting patterns of both sexism and racism and highlighted the absence of those lived experiences in feminist theory and literature. In a seminal publication, Crenshaw (1991) addressed this through line:

> In the context of violence against women, this elision of difference in identity politics is problematic, fundamentally because the violence that many women experience is often shaped by other dimensions of their identities, such as race and class. Moreover, ignoring difference within groups contributes to tension among groups, another problem of identity

> politics that bears on efforts to politicize violence against women. Feminist efforts to politicize experiences of women and antiracist efforts to politicize experiences of people of color have frequently proceeded as though the issues and experiences they each detail occur on mutually exclusive terrains. Although racism and sexism readily intersect in the lives of real people, they seldom do in feminist and antiracist practices. (p. 1242)

Crenshaw underscores the intersections of gender and race but also calls attention to the need to take into consideration the multidimensionality of identity when examining an individual's lived experience. Socioeconomic status, sexual orientation, gender identity, and immigration status, to name a few, should be accounted for when examining the individual's lived experience and the social structures and systemic oppression that grant some members of society unfair advantage while at the same time unfairly relegating others (Gerassi, 2015; Kelly, 2011; Crenshaw, 1991). The concept of intersectionality helps to illuminate why some individuals are more vulnerable than others to sex trafficking (Crawford, 2017). The acknowledgment of this vulnerability is essential, as addressed by Cook (2019), when examining the prosecution of sex traffickers, "The same inequality that creates the necessary preconditions for vulnerability to violence in the first instance, also obfuscates or masks power's pathology and compulsivity in the investigative and adjudicative processes" (p. 149). Intersectional theorists posit that these social structures, systems of oppression, and resulting public policies that create the conditions for these vulnerable populations to be unfairly relegated and exploited must be addressed and dismantled. Furthermore, these vulnerable populations must be empowered and incorporated into the process of addressing these inequities (Cook, 2019).

Intersectionality is a critical component within the literature that examines critical race theory (CRT) and its relationship to sex trafficking and sexual exploitation (Constance-Huggins et al., 2022; Butler, 2015). As a tenet of the theory, CRT examines the way our reality is socially constructed in a manner that positions racial minorities negatively, often associating them with the responsibilities of society's problems, more frequently than their White counterparts. Constance-Higgins and colleagues (2022) examined the negative social construction of Black girls who have been sex trafficked. This social construction includes dehumanization, being treated as adults and willing participants rather than victims, as well as their exclusion from sex trafficking awareness campaigns and the narrative surrounding sex trafficking victimization (Constance-Huggins et al., 2022). Social construction has deep roots in Western society, including the dehumanization and hyper-sexualization of Black women in the 1800s (Bravo, 2012). Butler (2015) examined the direct connection between the history of American slavery and sex trafficking, noting that "sexual stereotyping and commercial sexual exploitation were fundamental tools for enforcing Black slavery and, later, racial segregation and apartheid in the United States" (p. 125).

While this section barely skims the surface of available literature on CRT, intersectionality, and sex trafficking, it highlights the importance of considering multidimensionality of identity and the influence of social constructs by systems of oppression when reflecting on a survivor's lived experience. Holding these important contextual factors in mind may help providers offer more inclusive and affirming care to this vulnerable population.

## References


Bravo, K. E. (2012). *Black female "Things" in international law: A meditation on Saartjie Baartman and Truganini* I (Robert H. McKinney Sch. of Law, Legal Studies Research Paper No. 2012-25, 2012), http://papers.ssm.com/sol3/papers.cfm?abstract-id=2159002

Butler, C. N. (2015). A critical race feminist perspective on prostitution & sex trafficking in America. *Yale Journal of Law and Feminism, 27*, 95.

Cecchet, S. J., & Thoburn, J. (2014, September). The psychological experience of child and adolescent sex trafficking in the United States: Trauma and resilience in survivors. *Psychological Trauma: Theory, Research, Practice, and Policy, 6*(5), 482–493.

Chefetz, R. A. (2015). *Intensive psychotherapy for persistent dissociative processes: The fear of feeling real*. W.W. Norton & Company.

Cole, J., Sprang, G., Lee, R., & Cohen, J. (2016, January). The trauma of commercial sexual exploitation of youth: A comparison of CSE victims to sexual abuse victims in a clinical sample. *Journal of Interpersonal Violence, 31*(1), 122–146.

Constance-Huggins, M., Moore, S., & Slay, Z. M. (2022). Sex trafficking of black girls: A critical race theory approach topractice. *Journal of Progressive Human Services, 33*(1), 62–74.

Contreras, P. M., Kallivayalil, D., & Herman, J. L. (2017). Psychotherapy in the aftermath of human trafficking: Working through the consequences of psychological coercion. *Women & Therapy, 40*(1–2), 31–54.

Cook, B. B. (2019). Stop traffic: Using expert witnesses to disrupt intersectional vulnerability in sex trafficking prosecutions. *Berkeley Journal of Criminal Law, 24*, 147.

Crawford, M. (2017). International sex trafficking. *Women & Therapy, 40*(1–2), 101–122. https://doi.org/10.1080/02703149.2016.1206784

Crenshaw, K. (1991). Race, gender, and sexual harassment. *Sothern California Law Review, 65*, 1467.

Falcke, D., Boeckel, M., & Wagner, A. (2017). Intimate partner violence: Mapping the phenomenon in Rio Grande do Sul. *Psico, 48*(2), 120–129.

Ford, J. D., & Courtois, C. A. (2009). Defining and understanding complex trauma and complex traumatic stress disorders. In C. A. Courtois & J. D. Ford (Eds.), *Treating complex traumatic stress disorders: Scientific foundations and therapeutic models*. Guilford.

Gerassi, L. (2015). A heated debate: Theoretical perspectives of sexual exploitation and sex work. *Journal of Sociology and Social Welfare, 42*(4), 79.

Gold, S. N. (2000). *Not trauma alone: Therapy for child abuse survivors in family and social context*. Routledge.

Goldberg, A., & Moore, J. (2018, January). Domestic minor sex trafficking. *Child and Adolescent Psychiatric Clinics of North America, 27*(1), 77–92.

Herman, J. L. (1992a). Complex PTSD: A syndrome in survivors of prolonged and repeated trauma. *Journal of Traumatic Stress, 5*(3), 377–391.

Herman, J. L. (1992b). *Trauma and recovery: The aftermath of violence – From domestic abuse to political terror*. Basic Books.

Herman, J. L. (2003). Hidden in plain sight: Clinical reflections on prostitution. *Journal of Trauma Practice, 2*(3–4), 1–13.

Hopper, E. K., & Gonzalez, L. D. (2018). A comparison of psychological symptoms in survivors of sex and labor trafficking. *Behavioral Medicine, 44*(3), 177–188.

Hopper, E., & Hidalgo, J. (2006). Invisible chains: Psychological coercion of human trafficking victims. *Intercultural Human Rights Law Review, 1*, 185.

Hossain, M., Zimmerman, C., Abas, M., Light, M., & Watts, C. (2010, December). The relationship of trauma to mental disorder among trafficked and sexually exploited girls and women. *American Journal of Public Health, 100*(12), 2442–2449.

Howell, E. F. (2011). *Understanding and treating dissociative identity disorder: A relational approach*. Routledge.

Kelly, U. A. (2011). Theories of intimate partner violence: From blaming the victim to acting against injustice: Intersectionality as an analytic framework. *Advances in Nursing Science, 34*(3), E29–E51.

Kernberg, O. F. (1984). *Severe personality disorders: Psychotherapeutic strategies*. Yale University Press.

Kim, K. (2011). The coercion of trafficked workers. *Iowa Law Review, 96*(409), 409–474.

Lanctot, N., Reid, J. A., & Laurier, C. (2020, February). Nightmares and flashbacks: The impact of commercial sexual exploitation of children among female adolescents placed in residential care. *Child Abuse & Neglect, 100*, 104195.

Litam, S. D. A. (2017). Human sex trafficking in America: What counselors need to know. *Professional Counselor, 7*(1), 45–61.

McLeod, D. A., Havig, K., Natale, A., & Pharris, A. (2020). Intimate partner violence: Innovations in theory to inform clinical practice, policy, and research. *Social Sciences, 9*(5), 71.

Meshkovska, B., Siegel, M., Stutterheim, S. E., & Bos, A. E. R. (2015). Female sex trafficking: Conceptual issues, current debates, and future directions. *Journal of Sex Research, 52*(4), 380–395. https://doi.org/10.1080/00224499.2014.1002126

Nichols, A. J., Preble, K., & Cox, A. (2022). A state-level analysis of demographic characteristics and sex trafficking experiences of survivors. *Journal of Human Trafficking*, 1–18.

Oram, S., Khondoker, M., Abas, M., Broadbent, M., & Howard, L. M. (2015, December). Characteristics of trafficked adults and children with severe mental illness: A historical cohort study. *The Lancet Psychiatry, 2*(12), 1084–1091.

Ottisova, L., Hemmings, S., Howard, L. M., Zimmerman, C., & Oram, S. (2016, August). Prevalence and risk of violence and the mental, physical and sexual health problems associated with human trafficking: An updated systematic review. *Epidemiology and Psychiatric Sciences, 25*(4), 317–341.

Polaris Analysis of 2020 Data from the National Human Trafficking Hotline (2021) Retrieved 23 Feb 2021, From https://polarisproject.org/wp-content/uploads/2022/01/Polaris-Analysis-of-2020-Data-from-the-National-Human-Trafficking-Hotline.pdf

Putnam, F. W. (1989). *Diagnosis and treatment of multiple personality disorder*. The Guilford Press.

Putnam, F. W. (2016). *The way we are: How states of mind influence our identities, personality, and potential for change*. International Psychoanalytic Books.

Roe-Sepowitz, D. E., Hickle, K. E., Dahlstedt, J., & Gallagher, J. (2014). Victim or whore: The similarities and differences between victim's experiences of domestic violence and sex trafficking. *Journal of Human Behavior in the Social Environment, 24*(8), 883–898. https://doi.org/10.1080/10911359.2013.840552

Salami, T., Gordon, M., Coverdale, J., & Nguyen, P. T. (2018, March). What therapies are favored in the treatment of the psychological sequelae of trauma in human trafficking victims? *Journal of Psychiatric Practice, 24*(2), 87–96.

Seligman, M. E., & Beagley, G. (1975). Learned helplessness in the rat. *Journal of Comparative and Physiological Psychology, 88*(2), 534.

Walker, L. E. (1979). *The battered woman*. Harper & Row.

Walker, L. A. (1984). Battered women, psychology, and public policy. *American Psychologist, 39*(10), 1178.

Walker, L. E. (2016). *The battered woman syndrome*. Springer Publishing Company.

Wilson, K., Varcella, R., Brems, C., Benning, D., & Renfro, N. (1993). Levels of learned helplessness in abused women. *Women & Therapy, 13*(4), 53–67.

# Chapter 5
# Interventions

**Abstract** This chapter will comprise an organizing framework for trauma-informed practice with survivors of sex trafficking, guided by the three-phrase model for treating complex trauma, with an emphasis on safety and practical considerations, therapeutic relationship, skills acquisition, and considerations for trauma processing. Clinical recommendations for evidence-based practice will include an emphasis on the importance of interprofessional collaboration and service provision when working with this population.

**Keywords** Sex trafficking · Commercial sexual exploitation · CSE · Victim · Survivor · Intervention · Treatment · Therapy · Service(s) · PTSD · cPTSD · Trauma

## 5.1 Introduction

The sequelae of sex trafficking are often severe and chronic and span the medical/physical, psychological, occupational, and social domains (Duncan & Dehart, 2019). Though no specific evidence-based treatments have been developed or identified for survivors of commercial sexual exploitation (CSE; Hopper & Gonzalez, 2018), there are several evidence-based treatments that have been identified as relevant and helpful given the experiences of survivors and the symptoms and syndromes with which they tend to present (Marburger & Pickover, 2020; Salami et al., 2018).

A discussion of pathways out of trafficking and ways to engage survivors in psychotherapy and other types of treatment, though important, is beyond the scope of this chapter. The focus of this chapter will be treatment considerations and recommendations for survivors who have successfully made their way out of trafficking and are living in the community. It will also address some broader contextual

 
J. Davidtz et al., *Sex Trafficking*, SpringerBriefs in Psychology,
https://doi.org/10.1007/978-3-031-09120-9_5

considerations for the necessary resources and supports outside of therapy that survivors need in order to function and live independently

## 5.2 Common Clinical Symptoms and Syndromes

As discussed in the previous chapter, the most commonly experienced and documented psychological symptoms or diagnoses experienced by survivors of CSE include complex trauma, PTSD, dissociation, depression, anxiety, substance abuse, and suicidality (Cecchet & Thoburn, 2014; Cole et al., 2016; Lanctot et al., 2020; Oram et al., 2015; Ottisova et al., 2016). Survivors also live with overwhelming shame and profound disruptions in their sense of self and relatedness to others (Herman, 2003). Finally, they experience practical challenges and obstacles that hinder the process of recovery and reintegration and undermine their social and occupational functioning (Cole et al., 2016; Contreras et al., 2017; Meshkovska et al., 2015).

CSE survivors have typically endured severe trauma, often for long periods of time. In addition to the trauma they experience in the context of being trafficked, they often have histories of abuse and maltreatment and experience adversity in the form of being stigmatized and marginalized as they try to reintegrate. Another consequence of having been held captive is that they lack the skills and access to both the internal and external resources they need to function independently (O'Brien et al., 2019). For example, depending on how old they were when they were first trafficked and how long they were in captivity, they may never have learned basic skills that would allow them to manage money, to obtain and prepare food and other basic activities of daily living, or to find other needed resources like employment and childcare. For this reason, it is important for mental health providers to be aware of their other domains of need and to be prepared to collaborate with other providers to create a treatment and support network.

What follows is an outline of broad treatment considerations for survivors who have experienced the type of prolonged traumatization that constitutes sex trafficking. The central organizing recommendation is that it is essential to provide trauma-informed care to this population. A discussion of specific evidence-based treatments for different symptoms or diagnoses is beyond the scope of this chapter; however, evidence-based treatments that might be helpful in addressing the various problem or symptom domains will be referenced. The focus here is primarily on mental health needs and treatment; however, given the multifaceted nature of the challenges and difficulties CSE survivors live with, they need support in multiple domains, including housing; health, including mental health and substance abuse treatment; legal; and education and employment (Duncan & DeHart, 2019). Thus, recommendations for comprehensive services that address these different domains of need will be provided.

## 5.3 A Trauma-Informed Model for Psychotherapy with CSE Survivors

As noted above, there are several evidence-based treatments that are appropriate and effective for survivors of CSE. However, it is important to introduce a conceptual model for trauma-informed care according to which therapy can be structured and within which those treatments can be situated. The three-phase model that is widely recommended for treating complex posttraumatic stress disorder and associated conditions, like dissociative disorders, encompasses many of CSE survivors' needs and provides an intuitive and evidence-based structure within which to organize treatment (Courtois et al., 2009; Herman, 1992a, b; ISSTD, 2011). Since it is a conceptual model and not a theoretical orientation, it assumes and supports the responsive integration of a variety of evidence-based interventions according to each patient's needs while providing a predictable and safe holding space for containment of the patient's experience and the development and maintenance of a healing relationship.

It is important that conceptualizing treatment with CSE survivors according to an understanding of cPTSD and its phenomenological relevance to their experience be understood in terms of its value vis-à-vis acknowledging their subjective and practical needs, and not as a mechanism to further pathologize and stigmatize them. Furthermore, though not all CSE survivors present with cPTSD, this framework has practical utility and conceptual applicability in that it acknowledges the unique sequelae of having been in captivity and subjected to coercive control and the complexity of survivors' needs in recovering from traumatization to the degree of being able to function socially and occupationally. The diagnostic features of cPTSD were discussed in detail in the previous chapter, so this discussion will focus on the three-phase model of treatment that follows from the phenomenology of cPTSD.

Complex PTSD is characterized by disturbances in multiple domains, including a more complex and multiproblem symptom picture, disruptions in identity and relatedness, and vulnerability to repeated harm or traumatization. Treatment for complex PTSD takes place in three stages, each of which has a central task. The reader is referred to Herman (1992a, b), Courtois et al. (2009), and ISSTD (2011) for a detailed elucidation of the three-phase approach to treating complex PTSD. What follows is a conceptual overview of some of the key points that might help guide treatment planning.

### 5.3.1 *Phase 1: Safety and Stabilization*

CSE survivors may present with multiple threats to physical safety, including substance use, dissociation, and suicidal, or nonsuicidal self-injurious (NSSI), behavior (Cole et al., 2016). They may also be vulnerable to returning to their pimps or traffickers or being re-trafficked (Goldberg & Moore, 2018; O'Brien et al., 2019;

Salami et al., 2018) or be living in a situation where the threat of violence is still present. It is important to establish basic safety for treatment to be beneficial and for survivors to have the skills they need to tolerate and benefit from processing traumatic memories in the next phase. A relative degree of safety in terms of environment and emotion and behavior regulation is a prerequisite for progressing to phases 2 and 3 of treatment. Phase 1 is often the longest phase of treatment and one which some patients never move beyond but can benefit from as a continued source of support (Courtois et al., 2009).

The tasks of this phase are to support the survivor in establishing personal and interpersonal safety and developing the capacity to regulate arousal and affective states, provide psychoeducation, and support their sense of self and relational capacity (Courtois et al., 2009; Herman, 1992a, b). For some people, completing the tasks of phase 1 provides enough skills to manage posttraumatic symptoms, and the patient may not elect to do trauma processing in phase 2 for that or other reasons. However, once they have completed the tasks of this phase, they are still experiencing symptoms of PTSD, and they and their therapist can consider whether it would be appropriate to proceed to phase 2, of which processing traumatic memories is the primary task. Of note, beginning to process traumatic experiences can be destabilizing, and some patients benefit from moving back and forth between phase 1 and phase 2 as needed to refresh skills or revisit their safety plan (Courtois et al., 2009).

Phase 1 of treatment is the time period during which clinical symptoms associated with PTSD, depression, anxiety, dissociation, substance use, and suicidal or NSSI behavior should be addressed via employing appropriate evidence-based interventions, like cognitive behavior therapy, interpersonal therapy, and dialectical behavior therapy. It is important to note, however, that survivors of prolonged traumatization, including sex trafficking, present with high rates of treatment refractory anxiety and depression (Salami et al., 2018). Though evidence-based treatments can be helpful, severe anxiety and depression tend not to remit if the trauma background is not considered in the design and execution of treatment (Kinzie et al., 1990 in Herman, 1992a, b).

### *5.3.2 Phase 2: Processing of Traumatic Memories*

The primary task of this phase is to support the patient in developing and expressing a coherent autobiographical narrative account of their traumatic experience and its impact and integrating the trauma narrative into their overall narrative of themselves. In other words, the task is to develop a story of themselves that has complexity and nuance and is characterized by both enriching and uplifting experiences on the one hand and traumatic and tragic ones on the other hand (Courtois et al., 2009). There are several approaches to constructing or reconstructing the narrative, some of which do not prescribe or require recall of traumatic experiences. These approaches may be tolerated better than exposure-based approaches and are more appropriate for patients who are amnestic for some traumatic events or periods of time. The reader is referred to Courtois et al. (2009) for a discussion of some of those approaches.

This phase may also include trauma-processing approaches like prolonged exposure, cognitive processing therapy, or eye movement desensitization and reprocessing therapy. However, it is important to be sure the survivor is stable and has skills to avail themselves of in order to tolerate and benefit from such processing (Hardy et al., 2013; Salami et al., 2018). Ideally, this should be established collaboratively; however, if the therapist's assessment is that a patient is not ready for trauma processing in that they might be destabilized by it, they are advised to provide education and caution the patient to delay trauma processing until they are better able to benefit from it.

A key component of the work of this phase is to connect with and experience the emotions associated with traumatic memories. Unlike exposure treatments that tend to focus exclusively on anxiety, in the treatment of complex PTSD, patients are encouraged to experience a range of emotions, including grief and mourning, shame, and rage (Courtois et al., 2009). This phase may also include actions the patient takes in their relationships with others, including their abusers (e.g., confronting them). Given how activating and potentially destabilizing those actions and communications can be, there may be an intermittent need to pause and return to the safety and stabilization focus of phase one before resuming trauma processing.

### 5.3.3 *Phase 3: Reintegration*

The final phase of treatment, which can be seen as the culmination of the work of other phases and a time of celebration of gains, "…may also be fraught with difficulty for clients who have never had the opportunity for a life that is in the range of normal" (Courtois et al., 2009; p. 95). This phase of treatment might focus on ongoing issues in relationships and intimacy, sexual functioning, parenting, and career. During this phase, it is important to encourage the patient to develop and maintain a support system outside of the therapy relationship and to pursue other social and occupational goals.

## 5.4 Relational Considerations

Because being disempowered and disconnected from others are such core experiences of psychological trauma, recovery must necessarily include creating new connections, one of which is a therapeutic relationship (Herman, 1992ab; Contreras et al., 2017; Courtois et al., 2009). Core principles for recovery, which are employed within the context of what Herman terms a "healing relationship," include empowering the survivor and providing the opportunity to create new connections.

Survivors of sex trafficking have been subjected to coercive control, which is characterized in part by the perpetrator delivering both affection and cruelty (Contreras et al., 2017; Herman, 1992a, b; Herman, 2003). The traumatization that results from such experiences is relationally bewildering and may make the survivor as wary of warmth and kindness as they are of violence. This makes for a more complex than usual relational "dance" of psychotherapy and requires the trauma therapist to be especially mindful of the patient's cues in order to inform the most attuned response. It may also result in a very slow process – sometimes over a period of years – of coming to trust and feel safe with the therapist (Howell, 2011). In the case of survivors of sex trafficking, the challenges to developing trust and a sense of safety of the therapeutic space are compounded by the effects of shame, stigma, and secrecy that are perpetuated by living within a system of coercive control (Contreras et al., 2017; Herman, 1992a, b; Herman, 2003; Ijadi-Maghsoodi et al., 2016).

Though always important and characteristic of the unique nature of a therapy relationship, the importance of boundaries and predictability in the therapeutic relationship with trauma survivors cannot be overstated. The survivor must have the opportunity to experience the therapist as consistent and incorruptible. Traumatic transference enactments are not uncommon, and it is essential for therapists to be aware of their own reactions and to manage them therapeutically (Courtois et al., 2009; Dalenberg, 2000; Hayes et al., 2019; Herman, 1992a, b). Enactments may take the form of tests or invitations for the therapist to bend the treatment frame and make exceptions; however, if the therapist does so, rather than it being experienced as therapeutic, the therapist may be perceived as untrustworthy. Therapists who have a strong working conceptualization of the patient's attachment organization, are attuned to potential enactments, and have the capacity to manage their own anxiety will be in a better position to be responsive and to negotiate difficult choice points therapeutically (Hayes et al., 1992a, b).

## 5.5 Evidence-Based Psychotherapy Interventions

Various evidence-based interventions can be implemented within the phase-oriented framework described above to address symptoms and facilitate safety and improved social and occupational functioning. What follows is by no means an exhaustive list of all evidence-based interventions that are relevant to the presenting concerns of CSE survivors. However, the treatments briefly described here have been identified as having the most empirical support for alleviating symptoms and improving functioning in survivors of sex trafficking and thus as having some practical utility for practitioners trying to meet those individuals' needs.

### 5.5.1 Dialectical Behavior Therapy (DBT)

As discussed above, one of the primary tasks of phase one of the recommended phase-oriented treatment for survivors of complex trauma like CSE is developing the capacity to regulate emotional states. One of the most promising treatment approaches for this type of skills development is dialectical behavior therapy (DBT). DBT is a comprehensive treatment program and an evidence-based treatment for borderline personality disorder. Though DBT was first developed to treat individuals with chronic suicidality and suicidal and NSSI behavior, it has been demonstrated to be effective for a number of emotional and behavioral disturbances, including substance dependence (Cavicchiolia et al., 2019; McMain et al., 2007) and eating disorders (Wisniewski et al., 2007), and in outpatient (Comtois et al., 2007), inpatient (Swenson et al., 2007), and forensic (McCann et al., 2007) settings, with adults (Comtois et al., 2007; Linehan et al., 2007; McMain et al., 2007; Swenson et al., 2007), adolescents (Miller et al., 2007a, b; Rathus & Miller, 2016), and families (Fruzzetti et al., 2007).

DBT (Linehan, 1993) is designed to treat emotional and behavioral dysregulation via a synthesis of behavioral, mindfulness, and dialectical paradigms (Koerner & Dimeff, 2007; Linehan, 1993). The primary goals are to increase skillful behaviors, decrease unskillful behaviors, and support patients in building lives that feel worth living (Linehan, 1993, 2014). Standard DBT is structured and comprehensive and comprises four components: weekly individual therapy, weekly group skills training, between-session phone coaching for generalization of skills, and weekly consultation team meetings for the therapists. Standard DBT is recommended and beneficial for patients presenting with suicidal crises, severe self-injury, or other high-risk behaviors that are potentially life-threatening (some forms of substance use or eating disorders). However, for patients who are more stable and have attained basic safety, treatment that is less intensive, but still informed by some of the core treatment strategies, can be helpful and appropriate (Koerner, 2012).

The skills training component of DBT (Linehan, 2014) has been implemented widely for a range of clinical presentations (Valentine et al., 2015). Though methodological limitations make it difficult to assess the efficacy of this component as a standalone treatment, Valentine et al. (2015) noted some preliminary evidence supporting the use of DBT skills training as an effective treatment for a range of symptoms and difficulties. DBT skills training is organized into four modules that can be delivered independently or in series: (1) core mindfulness skills focus on supporting the capacity to be connected to one's body and the present moment; (2) emotion regulation skills focus on identifying, controlling, and modifying emotions; (3) distress tolerance skills focus on self-soothing strategies that are designed to endure crisis without resorting to ineffective coping strategies like NSSI, substance use, or other high-risk behaviors; and (4) interpersonal effectiveness skills support the capacity to get one's needs met in relationships (Linehan, 2014). Skills training can be offered in a group or individual format, and the practice and generalization of skills can be supported in individual therapy, via skills coaching with the therapist between sessions and via peer support.

### 5.5.2 Trauma-Focused CBT

Trauma-focused CBT (TF-CBT) is the most studied treatment for youth with PTSD (Ijadi-Maghsoodi et al., 2016). TF-CBT is a time-limited treatment approach that utilizes cognitive and behavioral treatment techniques with children and adolescents and their caregivers to treat trauma-related symptoms and other affective, cognitive, and behavioral difficulties resulting from, or associated with, trauma exposure.

Murray et al. (2008) describe the components of TF-CBT with traumatized youth according to the "PRACTICE" acronym: *p*sychoeducation and parenting skills, *r*elaxation, *a*ffective modulation, *c*ognitive processing, *t*rauma narrative, *i*n vivo desensitization, *c*onjoint child/parent sessions, *e*nhancing safety and future skills. A detailed discussion of TF-CBT is beyond the scope of this chapter, and the reader is referred to Murray et al. for a practical summary of each of these components, and their organization into three distinct phases that align with the recommended phase-oriented approach for individuals with complex posttraumatic conditions described above (Herman, 1992a, b; Courtois et al., 2009). Furthermore, in their useful elaboration on strategies for implementing trauma-focused CBT for youth with complex trauma, Cohen et al. (2012) note that there may be some added clinical benefit to extending the coping skills phase with a focus on safety and graded exposure, emphasizing relevant themes, and attending thoughtfully to termination in order to facilitate trust and a sense of safety.

### 5.5.3 Trauma-Processing Treatments

As noted above and discussed by several authors (e.g., Courtois et al., 2009; Hardy et al., 2013; Herman, 1992a, b; Salami et al., 2018), survivors of chronic traumatization, including survivors of sex trafficking, may benefit from trauma processing via evidence-based treatments like prolonged exposure (PE; Foa et al., 2007) or cognitive processing therapy (CPT; Resick et al., 2016). However, it is recommended that the decision to implement trauma processing be one that is made collaboratively between the patient and the therapist and is not initiated until the patient has adequate coping skills in place to be able to manage distress, physiological arousal, and emotion dysregulation such processing might induce.

### 5.5.4 *Substance Use Disorder Treatments*

Trafficking survivors often suffer from substance-related conditions. Substance use disorders might develop in an effort to cope with trauma and other symptoms, as a result of traffickers having used substances as one of several methods to exercise coercive control over their victims or both (Salami et al., 2018). Some of the treatment approaches that address psychiatric symptoms are also effective for addressing substance-related problems (e.g., DBT, McMain et al., 2007), and there are several treatments that are evidence-based for substance abuse specifically, including behavioral and cognitive therapies, family therapy, motivational interviewing, psychodynamic psychotherapy, and 12-step facilitation therapy (McGovern & Carroll, 2003).

In addition to psychotherapy, survivors presenting with substance-related disorders may benefit from 12-step groups or peer counseling (Duncan & Dehart, 2019), both in terms of supporting recovery or abstinence and providing additional social support. Finally, in the case of the need for acute treatment of dependency, inpatient or residential treatment might be indicated.

## 5.6 Pharmacotherapy

As noted above, survivors of CSE often experience intractable anxiety, depression, and posttraumatic symptoms. Though psychotherapy is considered the first-line treatment for those complaints, and severe depressive and anxious symptoms are unlikely to remit if trauma is not addressed in psychotherapy, adjunctive pharmacotherapy may be helpful (Salami et al., 2018).

There are several psychotropic medications that have demonstrated efficacy in treating some of the symptoms of PTSD, including mood stabilizers, anxiolytics, second-generation antipsychotics, and adrenergic blockers (Courtois et al., 2009; Opler et al., 2009). Psychotropic medications are most beneficially used in conjunction with psychotherapy, and patients with complex posttraumatic conditions tend to require more complex medication regimens. This is especially salient for patients who present with high risk for suicide attempt or substance use disorders, as lethality in overdose is a critical consideration in prescribing for them. Opler et al. note that the process of finding the right combination of medications with the right dosages may take longer and require close monitoring and management (2009). Therefore, it is important that pharmacological treatment be managed by a competent provider within a trauma-informed practice model and that there is transparency with the patient and among the members of the treatment team.

## 5.7 Medical Care

Women and girls who are commercially sexually exploited are exposed to significant medical and health risks, including pregnancies, abortions, and sexually transmitted infections, such as HIV/AIDS (Hardy et al., 2013). They also suffer significant physical and sexual injury during captivity that can have enduring medical consequences and require ongoing medical care. However, given that the trafficking situation has kept survivors isolated and disconnected from resources in the community, it can be a challenge for them to obtain and follow up on medical care. Therapists, case workers, and psychiatrists can be helpful in connecting them with medical services or coaching them in seeking out those services themselves. Survivors may also benefit from being connected with mentors who can help them access services (Hardy et al., 2013), and other survivors who have successfully exited sex trafficking and reintegrated can be especially helpful in navigating options and obtaining medical care and other resources (Ijadi-Maghsoodi et al., 2016).

## 5.8 Other Adjunctive Treatments and Programmatic Supports

Survivors of sex trafficking have often been so isolated and deprived by their captors that escaping the trafficking situation means entering a world that is unfamiliar to them and that they are poorly equipped to navigate. Their needs are significant, but the lack of community resources designed to meet those needs makes it difficult for even experienced trauma therapists to help them (Duncan & DeHart, 2019). Without the structural supports, it will be difficult for survivors to access and benefit from therapy, and without therapy, it will be difficult for survivors to gain mastery of the basic skills needed to function independently and support themselves and their children. For this reason, it is crucial that survivors have access to comprehensive services comprised of mental health and medical treatment, occupational support (including skills for activities of daily living and gainful employment; Crawford & Kaufman, 2008), housing support, and childcare.

The challenge of systemic limitations and the great need for more services notwithstanding, providers should collaborate to co-construct a treatment team that is cohesive, transparent, egalitarian, and survivor-centered in order to foster a sense of safety, support the acquisition of skills, and empower the survivor to utilize the supports available to them.

# References


Cavicchiolia, M., Movallia, M., Vassenaa, G., Ramellaa, P., Prudenziatia, F., & Maffeia, C. (2019). The therapeutic role of emotion regulation and coping strategies during a stand-alone DBT Skills training program for alcohol use disorder and concurrent substance use disorders. *Addictive Behaviors, 98*. https://doi.org/10.1016/j.addbeh.2019.106035

Cecchet, S. J., & Thoburn, J. (2014, September). The psychological experience of child and adolescent sex trafficking in the United States: Trauma and resilience in survivors. *Psychological Trauma: Theory, Research, Practice, and Policy, 6*(5), 482–493.

Cohen, J. A., Mannarinoa, A. P., Kliethermesb, M., & Murray, L. A. (2012). Trauma-focused CBT for youth with complex trauma. *Child Abuse Neglect, 36*(6), 528–541. https://doi.org/10.1016/j.chiabu.2012.03.007

Cole, J., Sprang, G., Lee, R., & Cohen, J. (2016, January). The trauma of commercial sexual exploitation of youth: A comparison of CSE victims to sexual abuse victims in a clinical sample. *Journal of Interpersonal Violence, 31*(1), 122–146.

Comtois, K. A., Koons, C. R., Kim, S. A., Manning, S. Y., Bellows, E., & Dimeff, L. A. (2007). Implementing standard dialectical behavior therapy in an outpatient setting. In L. A. Dimeff & K. Koerner (Eds.), *Dialectical behavior therapy in clinical practice: Applications across disorders and settings*. Guilford.

Contreras, P. M., Kallivayalil, D., & Herman, J. L. (2017). Psychotherapy in the aftermath of human trafficking: Working through the consequences of psychological coercion. *Women & Therapy, 40*(1–2), 31–54.

Courtois, C. A., Ford, J. D., & Cloitre, M. (2009). Best practices in psychotherapy for adults. In C. A. Courtois & J. D. Ford (Eds.), *Treating complex traumatic stress disorders: Scientific foundations and therapeutic models*. Guilford.

Crawford, M., & Kaufman, M. R. (2008, August). Sex trafficking in Nepal: Survivor characteristics and long-term outcomes. *Violence Against Women, 14*(8), 905–916.

Dalenberg, C. (2000). *Countertransference and the treatment of trauma*. American Psychological Association.

Duncan, A. C., & DeHart, D. (2019, May). Provider perspectives on sex trafficking: Victim pathways, service needs, & blurred boundaries. *Victims & Offenders, 14*(4), 510–531.

Foa, E. B., Hembree, E. A., & Rothbaum, B. O. (2007). *Prolonged exposure therapy for PTSD: Emotional processing of traumatic experiences: Therapist guide*. Oxford University Press.

Fruzzetti, A. E., Santisteban, D. A., & Hoffman, P. D. (2007). Dialectical behavior therapy with families. In L. A. Dimeff & K. Koerner (Eds.), *Dialectical behavior therapy in clinical practice: Applications across disorders and settings*. Guilford.

Goldberg, A., & Moore, J. (2018, January). Domestic minor sex trafficking. *Child and Adolescent Psychiatric Clinics of North America, 27*(1), 77–92.

Hardy, V. L., Compton, K. D., & McPhatter, V. S. (2013, February). Domestic minor sex trafficking: Practice implications for mental health professionals. *Journal of Women & Social Work, 28*(1), 8–18.

Hayes, J. A., Gelso, C. J., Kivlighan, D. M., & Goldberg, S. B. (2019). Managing countertransference. In *Psychotherapy relationships that work: Volume 1: Evidence-based therapist contributions* (3rd ed.). Oxford University Press.

Herman, J. L. (1992a). Complex PTSD: A syndrome in survivors of prolonged and repeated trauma. *Journal of Traumatic Stress, 5*(3), 377–391.

Herman, J. L. (1992b). *Trauma and recovery: The aftermath of violence – From domestic abuse to political terror*. Basic Books.

Herman, J. L. (2003). Hidden in plain sight: Clinical reflections on prostitution. *Journal of Trauma Practice, 2*(3–4), 1–13.

Hopper, E. K., & Gonzalez, L. D. (2018). A comparison of psychological symptoms in survivors of sex and labor trafficking. *Behavioral Medicine, 44*(3), 177–188.

Howell, E. F. (2011). *Understanding and treating dissociative identity disorder: A relational approach*. Routledge.

Ijadi-Maghsoodi, R., Cook, M., Barnert, E. S., Gaboian, S., & Bath, E. (2016, January). Understanding and responding to the needs of commercially sexually exploited youth: Recommendations for the mental health provider. *Child and Adolescent Psychiatric Clinics of North America, 25*(1), 107–122.

International Society for the Study of Trauma and Dissociation. (2011). Guidelines for treating dissociative identity disorder in adults, third revision. *Journal of Trauma & Dissociation, 12*(2), 115–187. https://doi.org/10.1080/15299732.2011.537247

Koerner, K. (2012). *Doing dialectical behavior therapy: A practical guide*. Guilford.

Koerner, K., & Dimeff, L. A. (2007). Overview of dialectical behavior therapy. In L. A. Dimeff & K. Koerner (Eds.), *Dialectical behavior therapy in clinical practice: Applications across disorders and settings*. Guilford.

Lanctot, N., Reid, J. A., & Laurier, C. (2020, February). Nightmares and flashbacks: The impact of commercial sexual exploitation of children among female adolescents placed in residential care. *Child Abuse & Neglect, 100*, 104195.

Linehan, M. M. (1993). *Cognitive-behavioral treatment of borderline personality disorder*. Guilford.

Linehan, M. M. (2014). *DBT skills training manual* (2nd ed.). Guilford.

Linehan, M. M., Bohus, M., & Lynch, T. R. (2007). Dialectical behavior therapy for pervasive emotion dysregulation. In J. Gross (Ed.), *Handbook of emotion regulation* (pp. 581–605). Guilford Press.

Marburger, K., & Pickover, S. (2020). A comprehensive perspective on treating victims of human trafficking. *The Professional Counselor, 10*(1), 13–24.

McCann, R. A., Ivanoff, A., Schmidt, H., & Beach, B. (2007). Implementing dialectical behavior therapy in residential settings with adults and juveniles. In L. A. Dimeff & K. Koerner (Eds.), *Dialectical behavior therapy in clinical practice: Applications across disorders and settings*. Guilford.

McGovern, M. P., & Carroll, K. M. (2003). Evidence-based practices for substance use disorders. *Psychiatric Clinics of North America, 26*(4), 991–1010.

McMain, S., Sayrs, J. H. R., Dimeff, L., & Linehan, M. M. (2007). Dialectical behavior therapy for individuals with borderline personality disorder and substance dependence. In L. A. Dimeff & K. Koerner (Eds.), *Dialectical behavior therapy in clinical practice: Applications across disorders and settings*. Guilford.

Meshkovska, B., Siegel, M., Stutterheim, S. E., & Bos, A. E. R. (2015). Female sex trafficking: Conceptual issues, current debates, and future directions. *Journal of Sex Research, 52*(4), 380–395. https://doi.org/10.1080/00224499.2014.1002126

Miller, A. L., Rathus, J. H., DuBose, A. P., Dexter-Mazza, E. T., & Goldklang, A. R. (2007a). Dialectical behavior therapy for adolescents. In L. A. Dimeff & K. Koerner (Eds.), *Dialectical behavior therapy in clinical practice: Applications across disorders and settings*. Guilford.

Miller, A. L., Rathus, J. H., & Linehan, M. M. (2007b). *Dialectical behavior therapy with suicidal adolescents*. Guilford.

Murray, L. K., Cohen, J. A., Ellis, B. H., & Mannarino, A. (2008). Cognitive behavioral therapy for symptoms of trauma and traumatic grief in refugee youth. *Child and Adolescent Psychiatric Clinics of North America, 17*, 585–604.

O'Brien, J. E., Jordan, B., Honeycutt, N., Wilsnack, C., & Davison, C. (2019). "It's all about breaking down those barriers…": Exploring survivors' perspectives on services and treatment needs following commercial sexual exploitation during childhood. *Journal of Evidence-Based Social Work, 16*(2), 160–177.

Opler, L. A., Grennan, M. S., & Ford, J. D. (2009). Pharmacotherapy. In C. A. Courtois & J. D. Ford (Eds.), *Treating complex traumatic stress disorders: Scientific foundations and therapeutic models*. Guilford.

Oram, S., Khondoker, M., Abas, M., Broadbent, M., & Howard, L. M. (2015, December). Characteristics of trafficked adults and children with severe mental illness: A historical cohort study. *The Lancet Psychiatry, 2*(12), 1084–1091.

Ottisova, L., Hemmings, S., Howard, L. M., Zimmerman, C., & Oram, S. (2016, August). Prevalence and risk of violence and the mental, physical and sexual health problems associated with human trafficking: An updated systematic review. *Epidemiology and Psychiatric Sciences, 25*(4), 317–341.

Rathus, J. J., & Miller, A. L. (2016). *DBT skills manual for adolescents*. Guilford.

Resick, P. A., Monson, C. M., & Chard, K. M. (2016). *Cognitive processing therapy for PTSD: A comprehensive manual*. Guilford.

Salami, T., Gordon, M., Coverdale, J., & Nguyen, P. T. (2018, March). What therapies are favored in the treatment of the psychological sequelae of trauma in human trafficking victims? *Journal of Psychiatric Practice, 24*(2), 87–96.

Swenson, C. R., Witterholt, S., & Bohus, M. (2007). Dialectical behavior therapy on inpatient units. In L. A. Dimeff & K. Koerner (Eds.), *Dialectical behavior therapy in clinical practice: Applications across disorders and settings*. Guilford.

Valentine, S. E., Bankoff, S. M., Poulin, R. M., Reidler, E. B., & Pantalone, D. W. (2015). The use of dialectical behavior therapy skills training as stand-alone treatment: A systematic review of the treatment outcome literature. *Journal of Clinical Psychology, 71*(1), 1–20.

Wisniewski, L., Safer, D., & Chen, E. (2007). Dialectical behavior therapy and eating disorders. In L. A. Dimeff & K. Koerner (Eds.), *Dialectical behavior therapy in clinical practice: Applications across disorders and settings*. Guilford.

# Chapter 6
# Cultural Considerations

**Abstract** This chapter examines cultural considerations applicable to sex trafficking worldwide with an emphasis on multicultural victims detected in the United States. Data, risk factors, and systemic barriers relevant to multicultural victims of sex trafficking are provided. This chapter also covers disparities in sex trafficking experiences between diverse populations of domestic and foreign nationals who are exploited for commercial sex in the United States. Transcultural, trauma-informed adaptations to victim assessment and treatment are also suggested.

**Keywords** Transcultural · Diversity · Immigration

## 6.1 Introduction

Domestic and foreign national victims of sex trafficking have been detected across all 50 United States and the District of Columbia (United Nations Office on Drugs and Crime [UNODC], 2018). Individuals trafficked for commercial sex were identified among legitimate and illegal businesses involving a variety of facades, such as hospitality, travel, agriculture, domestic work, drug smuggling, and child care. Victims were also trafficked across rural and metropolitan areas (Cole & Sprang, 2015; Le et al., 2018). The US Department of Homeland Security (USDHS) investigated 947 cases of human trafficking in 2020, and the Department of Justice (DOJ) formally opened 663 human trafficking investigations within the same year. A large majority of DOJ investigations of human trafficking in 2020 comprised predominately of sex trafficking (i.e., 619 cases), while only 3 cases involved trafficking for both sex and labor (USDOS, 2021). Moreover, annual data revealed adult females constituted the majority of trafficking victims detected nationally (UNODC, 2012; USDOS, 2021).

Modern advancements have undoubtedly facilitated the expansion of human trafficking as exemplified by the majority of sex trafficking transactions involving minor age females initated on the Internet (Mitchell et al., 2011; UNODC, 2012). An increase in national and transnational cases of sex trafficking occurred as

 
J. Davidtz et al., *Sex Trafficking*, SpringerBriefs in Psychology,
https://doi.org/10.1007/978-3-031-09120-9_6

technology advances permitted persons from differing regions access to rising global markets (Dandurand, 2017; Farrell & Pfeffer, 2014; Lee, 2011; Mitchell et al., 2011). For example, detected victims from Southeast Asia were exploited in Australia and Japan, with traffickers profiting between $10,000 and $15,000 per victim. Meanwhile, foreign national and domestic persons were involved in trafficking transactions of up to $100,000 recorded in the United States (UNODC, 2020).

## 6.2 Global Statistics

In general, female victims were trafficked more frequently than their male counterparts (UNODC, 2020, 2021a). Global statistics accounting for persons trafficked in 2018 noted 50% of victims detected were trafficked for sex, and of every ten victims detected, five were adult females and two were minor age females (UNODC, 2018). Moreover, 20% of detected victims were identified as adult males, and nearly one-third comprised male and female children (UNODC, 2020). The United Nations also recorded trafficking victim demographics between different regions of the world. In low-income countries, half of the victims detected were children. While the majority of victims detected in sub-Saharan African countries were also children, adults accounted for a much greater percentage of victims in Eastern Europe and Central Asia (UNODC, 2020). Furthermore, the US Department of State (USDOS, 2021) revealed 11 governments worldwide (i.e., Afghanistan, Burma, China, Cuba, Eritrea, Korea, North Iran, Russia, South Sudan, Syria, Turkmenistan) documented practices of human trafficking that were linked to official operations (e.g., government-funded programs, government-affiliated services).

## 6.3 North America

According to the UNODC (2020), 72% of human trafficking victims detected in North America (i.e., the United States, Canada, Mexico) since 2018 were mainly exploited for commercial sex. Moreover, 25% of trafficked persons in the region were identified as migrants, and at least 50% of overall victims were targeted through their economic need (UNODC, 2020). North America was observed as one of the few destinations hosting a significant percentage of victims detected as persons trafficked from other regions, ranking behind Western and Southern Europe, and the affluent countries in the Middle East (UNODC, 2020). In 2017, the National Human Trafficking Hotline (2020) reported 57% of potential victims of human trafficking were national citizens or lawful permanent residents, while 43% were identified as undocumented. Relatedly, several trafficking victims migrated willingly, while others relocated against their will (USDOS, 2021). In 2019, the United States, Mexico, and Honduras ranked top three countries of origin of federally identified victims (USDOS, 2020). Consequently, victims of sex trafficking detected in the

United States were often accustomed to cultural backgrounds and perspectives that differed from the environmental contexts of their destinations.

Although a large number of individuals trafficked were foreigners to the United States, the majority of victims detected nationally were domestic citizens (UNODC, 2018). US citizen females accounted for the majority of victims across 78 cases of trafficking through *remote interactive sexual acts* occurring via webcams, chats, and phone lines, and minors were victimized in just under half of those cases (Polaris, 2019). While Hispanic (18%) and Black (12%) individuals accounted for a larger portion of the overall US population, Asian Americans (6%) encompassed the fastest growing racial or ethnic group in the nation. Moreover, one study found no differences in risk related to race across 814 victims of commercial sexual exploitation (CSE) and domestic minor sex trafficking (O'Brien et al., 2017), although several others evidenced a greater risk for African American females than White females overall (Cecchet & Thoburn, 2014; Fedina et al., 2019; Naramore et al., 2017). The Trafficking Victims Protection Act (TVPA) and subsequent policy changes regarding sexual exploitation in the United States accelerated a shift in public attention and general funding from victims of international trafficking to victims of domestic origin (UNODC, 2020). However, the COVID-19 pandemic increased human trafficking conducted online and simultaneously deterred response-related efforts (UNODC, 2021b; Polaris, 2019).

## 6.4 Cultural Considerations Within Process

The American Psychological Association (APA, 2020) defines *culture* as:

> (1) The distinctive customs, values, beliefs, knowledge, art, and language of a society or a community. These values and concepts are passed on from generation to generation, and they are the basis for everyday behaviors and practices. (2) The characteristic attitudes and behaviors of a particular group within society, such as a profession, social class, or age group. (p.1)

These definitions consider systemic influences that impact aspects of identity and group experience. The USDOS (2020) listed cultural groups in the United States that were vulnerable to human trafficking. The list included groups of persons with limited English proficiency, those belonging to immigrant groups (e.g., asylees, migrant laborers, participants of visa programs, foreign national domestic workers, undocumented individuals), American Indians, and Alaska Natives. Additionally, children dependent of state welfare or juvenile justice systems and persons exposed to mental health-related difficulties (i.e., disabilities, domestic violence, substance abuse) were also considered vulnerable to human trafficking (Fedina et al., 2019; Haney et al., 2020; Jaeckl & Laughon, 2021; Le et al., 2018; USDOS, 2020).

The United States, Jamaica, the Netherlands, and Japan all comprised major commercial sex markets considered to elicit sexual exploitation (APA, 2014). Researchers alluded to a cultural tolerance for sex trafficking in the United States that supported transnational operations (APA, 2014; Haney et al., 2020). Meanwhile, the DOS warned its audience of fabricated narratives regarding sex trafficking that are strategically disseminated by national extremist groups (e.g., White supremacists) to grow membership and power (USDOS, 2021).

Data accounting for 405 sex trafficking cases in the United States for *personal sexual servitude*, between December 2007 and December 2016, revealed that a greater majority of victims conveyed US citizenship (39%) as compared to those identified as foreign nationals (36%; Polaris, 2019). More adults (74%) were found sold than minors (30%), and victims were identified as males (15%), females (87%), or a gender minority (less than 1%). These individuals were identified as trafficked for the explicit purpose of engaging in nonconsensual sex over an extended period of time, and several experienced non-consenting marriage situations (Polaris, 2019). The detected victims of personal sexual servitude arrived predominantly from Mexico and Central America, while several reported Southeast Asian origins.

Moreover, domestic minor victims were more likely to be of a minority race or ethnicity and to have migrated from their homes (Fedina et al., 2019). Of 115 child sex trafficking victims studied by Fedina et al. (2019) in one Midwestern state, 65.2% identified as Black or African American, 3.5% endorsed Hispanic ethnicity, and 26.1% reported being White. Notably, no group differences were observed with regard to age, race or ethnicity, gender, and income between adults who were victims of child sex trafficking and non-trafficked adults engaged in commercial sex (Fedina et al., 2019). However, the authors also reported that children of a racial minority were twice as likely to be victimized for commercial sex as White children.

### 6.4.1 US Culture of Authority

Human trafficking offenses occurring within the United States are primarily investigated by the DOJ, DHS, and Department of State (DOS). Additionally, the Federal Bureau of Investigation (FBI) participates by collecting data on state and local cases (FBI, 2021; UNODC, 2018). In 2019, DHS initiated 1024 cases related to human trafficking. Of those investigations, 208 involved sex trafficking. In 2018, the US Department of Justice (DOJ) successfully prosecuted 454 traffickers who were predominantly involved in sex trafficking. Yet, it is pertinent to acknowledge that US legal officials not only prosecuted traffickers; they also charged trafficking victims for crimes committed under coercion (Dandurand, 2017; Farrell & Pfeffer, 2014). The research evidenced that anti-trafficking initiatives were impacted by policies and investigative efforts to criminalize individuals at increased risk of being sexually trafficked, such as migrants (Sabon, 2018), sex workers (Dandurand, 2017; Dandurand & Chin, 2014; Farley et al., 2016; Turner et al., 2021), and child victims (Cecchet & Thoburn, 2014; USDOS, 2021).

#### 6.4.1.1 Sex Trafficking Among Members of Authority

Criticism has grown over the United States' internationalization of law enforcement through installation of military camps known to host sex workers within communities exposed to high rates of organized crime and radical political leadership (Dandurand & Chin, 2014; Lee, 2011). Individuals across highly ranked positions of power assigned by the US government, such as Naval and Army reserve officers, state attorneys, and members of law enforcement, have been reported to either sexually traffic or engage in sexual acts with victims (USDOS, 2021). Cases of human trafficking involving US military members are investigated by the Department of Defense (DOD). The DOD reported investigating 37 total cases between 2014 and 2016 (UNODC, 2018). A significant increase in cases was observed by the DOD in 2020, which comprised 160 investigations of human trafficking perpetrated by military, civilian, and contracted personnel (UNODC, 2018). The FBI's *Color of Law* was established to safeguard victims exposed to abuse of authority by members of local, state, or federal government (e.g., officers, prosecutors, judges; FBI, n.d.). Sexual assault occurring on or off duty was specified within the Color of Law criteria.

#### 6.4.1.2 Response Efforts by Members of Authority

The FBI contributed to bridging gaps between local law enforcement agencies and victim reports of human trafficking. It classified commercial sex acts as those during which an adult is induced, forced, frauded, or coerced to participate or in which the person induced is below 18 years old (Lauger & Durose, 2021). In 2013, the FBI put forth efforts to improve its communications with local police agencies by establishing its Uniform Crime Reporting-Human Trafficking (UCR-HT) data collection tool (FBI, 2021). The UCR-HT has since been used to track data relevant to cases of coerced commercial sex acts (e.g., sex trafficking) and voluntary servitude (e.g., labor trafficking; FBI, 2021).

Of the 47 states who participated in the UCR-HT data collection for 2020, 31 states reported at least 1 arrest for human trafficking, and 19 states reported between 1 and 10 arrests for sex trafficking. Meanwhile, Texas and Georgia each reported over 25 arrests (Lauger & Durose, 2021). Of the participating local law enforcement agencies, 155 agencies reported between 2 and 10 sex trafficking offenses in 2020, 27 agencies reported between 11 and 100 sex trafficking offenses, and 2 agencies reported 101 or more (Lauger & Durose, 2021). Moreover, 301 arrests for human trafficking involving commercial sex acts took place in 2020 across all participating states (Lauger & Durose, 2021).

The federal government also funds victim assistance programs providing case management and service referrals (e.g., medical, dental, mental health, substance use treatment, shelter, legal aid, employment, transportation) to victims. In 2017, a total of 1736 domestic (636) and foreign national (1100) victims of trafficking were provided case management services through the Department of Health and Human

Services (HHS; UNODC, 2018). Moreover, the DOJ funded $4.7 million toward specialized services and mentorship opportunities for minor age victims of sex trafficking and sexual exploitation in 2019 (USDOS, 2021). Between 2016 and 2017, HHS issued 1730 Certification and Eligibility Letters for foreign national adult and children victims to become eligible for comprehensive services and benefits (USDOS, 2020). Of the 508 foreign national adult victims certified in 2020, 15% were sex trafficking victims, and 11% were victims of both sex and labor trafficking (UNODC, 2021a). Of 673 foreign national child victims certified in 2020, 25% were sex trafficking victims, and 5% were victims of both labor and sex trafficking (UNODC, 2021a).

Fortunately, more traffickers were brought to justice throughout the years. Globally, the number of people convicted nearly tripled since 2003, which may be credited to anti-trafficking legislation and to the national and international defenses employed to strengthen federal practices (UNODC, 2020). Moreover, a rise in domestic victims of sex trafficking detected in the United States has amplified service providers' awareness, training, and dissemination of information to the public (Dandurand, 2017; Helton, 2016).

#### 6.4.1.3 Victim Experiences with Members of Authority

It would be neglectful to overlook the heightened pressure applied on foreign victims of sex trafficking arriving into the United States between 2016 and 2020. During that period of time, the US administration intensified anti-immigration policies and practices, increased law enforcement against undocumented persons, and expanded military presence at the southern border (Ford-Paz et al., 2020; Sisson, 2018). Moreover, the current government's implementation of policies impeding access to immigration relief for trafficked individuals increased foreign national victims' fear for their safety. For example, the pandemic-related Title 42 order of the Public Health Service Act, established in March 2020, led to the prompt removal of asylum seekers at the border, the hold of unaccompanied minors by DHS, and the separation of several families in the process (Vilches Hinojosa et al., 2021).

Child victims were found especially vulnerable to authoritarian practices in the United States, considering they were prosecuted for prostitution in 19 states, despite protections established by federal law. Eighteen states reported implementation of laws to protect minors from prosecution for certain crimes (e.g., theft, forgery) excluding those indicating involvement in commercial sex (USDOS, 2021). Consequently, skepticism for the criminal justice system and persons enforcing its practices has festered among those documented and undocumented in the United States despite institutional response efforts. Additional cultural factors were found relevant to the underreporting of human trafficking victims, such as the culture established by the local police agencies (Farrell & Pfeffer, 2014; Lee, 2011) and officer perspectives of sexual exploitation (UNODC, 2021b; Farrell & Pfeffer, 2014; Haney et al., 2020).

Following interviews of police officers, prosecutors, victim service providers, and legal personnel involved in investigations of human trafficking, Farrell and

Pfeffer (2014) identified a lack of investigative culture and systemic organization. The authors particularly noted agency difficulty detecting and responding to diverse types of cases involving human trafficking in their communities. Local law enforcement officers from 12 respective counties in the United States approached sex trafficking situations as they would traditional crimes. Moreover, officers attributed underreporting to victim reluctance to self-identify as a person being trafficked for sex and the victims' fear of police and their traffickers (Farrell & Pfeffer, 2014).

### *6.4.2 Culturally Relevant Conflicts Experienced by Victims*

Internet expansion has facilitated recruitment and communications between commercial traffickers, further diversifying the backgrounds of both traffickers and victims (Lee, 2011; Polaris, 2019; UNODC, 2021a). Therefore, implications of diversity inevitably arise among individual victims of sex trafficking who express specific cultural beliefs. For example, female trafficking victims reported inability to access formal justice systems involving male judicial officials due to cultural norms precluding their engagement with those of the opposite gender (APA, 2014). Relatedly, female sex trafficking victims who accessed services in foreign nations were penalized for "moral crimes," such as having sex outside of marriage (Brown, 2021). Women of Latino origins were frequently observed to assume a submissive role when victimized by violence, which often led them to tolerate abusive treatment and downplay their distress (Cuevas et al., 2012; Murshid & Bowen, 2018; Sabon, 2018; Sisson, 2018; Zadnik et al., 2016). Similar accounts of submissive obedience were reported for Black (Chen, 2010) and Asian (Chen, 2010; Hwang, 2021) victims.

An analysis of 6 years' worth (i.e., 2006–2011) of cases against 382 total traffickers revealed that victims were more likely to be trafficked by someone in their own communities and of the same race, migrant status, and gender (Denton, 2016). Furthermore, of 2448 victims of sex trafficking situations in the United States throughout 2020, 42% were recruited by a family member, and 39% were recruited by their intimate partner or through a marriage proposition (Polaris, 2022). Lee (2011) attributed an increase in abuse of tourist and marriage visas in South Korea to the criminalization of human trafficking by way of commercial sex. In 2020, cases of child trafficking through marriage doubled in Cambodia, with victims as young as 14 years old detected. Similar trends were observed in Brazil, Nepal, and Southern India, while researchers ascribed the surge in child marriage victims to mass employment losses caused by the COVID-19 pandemic and related pressure to assist their families (UNODC, 2021b). In addition to coerced marriage, forced use of substances, nonconsensual sex leading to pregnancy, and involuntary abortions were deemed consequences of sex trafficking (Lederer & Wetzel, 2014) thatconflicted with the religious and cultural values of victims.

Along with their increased risk of exposure to sex trafficking, several underserved populations have also been found more likely to go undetected. Black persons (APA, 2014; Brown, 2021; Butler, 2015), members of LGBTQ communities (APA, 2014; DeBoise, 2012; Polaris, 2019; UNODC, 2018, 2020), individuals engaged in sex work (Dandurand, 2017; Farrell & Pfeffer, 2014; Gerassi, 2015; Ottisova et al., 2016; Polaris, 2019), and immigrants (Nsonwu, 2019; UNODC, 2021a; USDOS, 2020) were all repeatedly found to underreport their sex trafficking experiences to law enforcement.

Brown (2021) challenged societal perceptions of minor Black females being "more adult and less innocent" than minor White females, attributing such viewpoint to the disparity in harsher discipline provided to Black females by educators, law enforcement, and other authorities. Racial disparity across education, job opportunities, and other influencers of financial status (e.g., generational wealth) facilitate traffickers' use of resources to entice their victims (APA, 2014; Brown, 2021; UNODC, 2020). Unfortunately, the disproportionate effect of COVID-19 on Black persons' health was observed as an additional factor contributing to their increased risk of human trafficking (UNODC, 2021b). Moreover, Black females accounted for 13.4% of the general population, 40% of detected sex trafficking victims, and nearly 60% of juvenile prostitution arrests in 2020 (Brown, 2021).

### *6.4.3 United States Immigration Status*

US immigrants are defined as persons who seek to remain in the United States for an indefinite period of time, whether for residency, citizenship, or employment (United States Citizenship and Immigration Services [USCIS], 2020b). The foregoing description comprises lawful permanent residents, refugees and asylees, immigrants with special status, and those undocumented. Individuals who hold a transitory residency (e.g., tourists, international students, performers) are not considered immigrants; however, they are exposed to risk during their short-term stay nevertheless (USCIS, 2020b). Several victims of sex trafficking become immigrants during their exploitation, while others are trafficked post-migration.

#### 6.4.3.1 Immigration in the United States

Since 1990, the US immigration population has more than doubled, constituting 44.8 million individuals or roughly 13.7% of the nation's population (Budiman et al., 2020). The Executive Office for Immigration Review (EOIR), a sub-agency of the Department of Justice, oversees US immigration courts enforcing proceedings relevant to admissibility and removability of persons entering the United States (Barber & Garcia, 2019). Many foreign national individuals lack understanding of legal practices in the United States including immigration-related procedures. Moreover, mandated practices increase social pressures to integrate in the communities they migrated to (Ahmed & Rasmussen, 2020; Barber & Garcia, 2019; Kim et al., 2019).

Asia accounted for the most prevalent population of immigrants arriving in the United States in 2018 (Batalova et al., 2020; Budiman et al., 2020). Moreover, Mexican-origin immigrants made up the largest immigrant group as compared to other Hispanic and Latino immigrant groups (Batalova et al., 2020). Currently, immigrants originating from Mexican and Central American parts account for 67% of the undocumented immigrant population (Batalova et al., 2020).

#### 6.4.3.2 Trafficking of Immigrants in the United States

Although sex trafficking in the United States does not exclusively occur among immigrated individuals, it is evident that they constitute a large percentage of those accounted for by national human trafficking statistics. "Migration/relocation" was the fifth most prevalent risk factor observed across National Human Trafficking Hotline (NHTH) reports of sex trafficking in 2020 (Polaris, 2022). Sex traffickers recruiting, transporting, and exploiting foreign and domestic individuals ranged from lone perpetrators to organized crime networks (APA, 2014; UNODC, 2018, 2020). Refugees, undocumented individuals, and their families faced increased risk of danger from criminal individuals or organizations involved in their migration (APA, 2014; Nsonwu, 2019; van Veldhuizen et al., 2017). The DOJ reported 9854 cases of trafficking initiated between July 1, 2019, and June 30, 2020, noting that 62% of individuals served were victims of sex trafficking and 7% were identified as trafficked for both sex and labor. A reported 61% of those served were US citizens or lawful permanent residents, while 37% were foreign nationals, and the status of 2% was unknown (UNODC, 2021a).

California (10.6 million), Texas (five million), Florida (4.5 million), and New York (4.4 million) constituted the top four states to host the largest numbers of individuals arriving from other countries in 2019 (Batalova et al., 2020). Remarkably, California (4970), Texas (3559), Florida (2539), and New York (1739) were also the top four states with the largest number of tip reports regarding human trafficking (NHTH, 2020). Tip reports were collected again in 2020 via phone calls, text, WebChats, emails, or online, and a total of 51,667 substantive tip reports were received nationwide (NHTH, 2020). Besides, evidence-based predictions supported that hotline estimates of trafficking situations are likely to rise (Brown, 2021; NHTH, 2020), which were reinforced by a near 40% increase observed since the beginning of the COVID-19 pandemic (UNODC, 2020).

#### 6.4.3.3 United States Immigration Relief

US asylum eligibility standards require an individual to establish a history of persecution or fear of persecution as a result of the immigrant's "race, religion, nationality, political opinion or membership in a particular social group" (USCIS, 2020b, p.1). Therefore, immigration officials often work with victims of sex trafficking and related crimes to determine whether they qualify for immigration relief (Murshid &

Bowen, 2018), such as the *T nonimmigrant status* (T visa). The T visa is a temporary (i.e., 4-year period) immigration benefit uniquely offered to noncitizen victims of severe human trafficking in the United States. The purpose of the T visa is to facilitate law enforcement's investigation and prosecution of those who committed human trafficking-related crimes.

Individuals granted T visa status must remain in the states, comply with reasonable investigative measures, and report anticipation of extreme hardship by unusual and severe danger associated with their removal from the United States. Victims under 18 years old and those who experienced trauma-related difficulty that impedes their ability to comply are exempt from participating in official investigations. Benefits of a T visa include opportunities to sponsor relatives who are also at risk of danger, authorization to gain employment, and eligibility for federal benefits and services (United States Department of State [USDOS], 2020). T visa recipients were also eligible to request lawful permanent resident status and ultimately citizenship.

There were 5000 visas available for request by those who were victims of human trafficking in 2019, and the annual cap has not been reached to date (USDHS, 2020). In 2020, there appeared to be an increase in the number of victims granted T nonimmigrant status ($n$ = 1040) compared to the previous year ($n$ = 500). An opposite trend was observed in 2019, during which DHS granted 76 T visas less than it did in 2018 (UNODC, 2018). Remarkably, application processing times had increased from 12.1 months in 2018 to 18.6 month in 2020 (USDOS, 2021). Additionally, a decrease in overall use of services was reported in 2020 albeit increased government funding for the fiscal year (USDOS, 2020). Immigrated victims trafficked by a US citizen or lawful permanent resident also sought relief through the Violence Against Women Act (VAWA) of 1994, which protects victims of battery or extreme cruelty perpetrated by individuals with legal status in the United States (USCIS, 2020a).

The *U nonimmigrant status* (i.e., U visa) is another immigration benefit offered to victims of certain qualifying crimes, such as human trafficking, and has been helpful to agencies combating related criminal activities (USCIS, 2018). Of note, the federal government has also offered a shorter-term stay through its granting of a *Continued Presence* (CP) status, which, unlike the longer-term visas, expires and requires renewal at 1-year increment (DHS, 2010). The purpose of CP is to allow immigrated victims temporary residence in the United States; meanwhile, authorities investigate the crimes committed against them (DHS, 2010; USDOS, 2021). DHS granted Continued Presence to 117 trafficking victims in 2020 (USDOS, 2021).

Although specific immigration referral actions (e.g., T visa, U visa, VAWA) require an assessment of victim exposure to traumatic events, which frequently include events directly related to sex trafficking (Garcini et al., 2017), DHS has repeatedly denied T visa applications containing disclosures of complex trauma (e.g., domestic violence, sexual exploitation during smuggling; UNODC, 2021a). Whether legal relief is granted to an individual has remained a determination of immigration courts. Nevertheless, a thorough psychological assessment and record of immigrant experiences may greatly influence legal results (Baranowski, 2020; Barber & Garcia, 2019).

Advocates for undocumented individuals oppose several changes implemented by those responding to victims and situations of sex trafficking, such as adjudicators' increased requests for additional evidence, delayed processing times, and visa denials based on what advocates perceived to be reasons of wrongful interpretation (Dandurand, 2017). For example, visas were denied to victims whose traffickers obligated them to engage in criminal acts due to the victim's involvement in the illegal activity (Dandurand, 2017; Monga et al., 2014). Moreover, the UNODC (2021b) noted worsened and novel challenges regarding victim access to public services.

## 6.5 Cultural Considerations for Clinical Work

Due to the national and international patterns of human trafficking for sexual exploitation, victims express a multitude of respective diverse backgrounds. Therefore, cultural considerations must apply when working with these individuals. Such considerations include implications of ethnicity-based experiences, cultural values, and linguistic knowledge.

The fifth edition of the DSM-5 (APA, 2013) is indispensable when clinically diagnosing individuals in the United States. The diagnostic manual includes sections that focus on the assessment of diverse populations. A cultural formulation interview (CFI; APA, 2013), which lists questions that aid in gathering information regarding clinical symptoms and cultural affects that influence diagnostic opinions, is located on pages 750 through 757 of the DSM-5. However, the clinical manual does not sufficiently account for immigrant experiences, and it fails to acknowledge cross-cultural and diverse responses to repeated trauma (Kimmell et al., 2020; Wylie et al., 2018). Service providers who are qualified and requested to provide their diagnostic impressions of multicultural victims should consider broadening their diagnostic competence. Doing so prevents mischaracterization of culturally appropriate behaviors as criteria of mental illness and strengthens awareness of material that is clinically pertinent.

With respect to treatment, experts caution the use of traditional North American practices to address the mental health needs of multicultural victims (Bryant-Davis & Gobin, 2019; Dewan, 2014; Hershberger, 2021; Rafferty, 2018; Rajan & Bryant-Davis, 2021). Specific alternatives to traditional Western therapies were suggested for working with victims who emigrated from South and Southeast Asia, particularly the use of holistic healing modalities (e.g., spiritual rituals, massage therapy, acupuncture, deep breathing, meditation, herbal gardening, yoga) to assess the mind-body relationship across issues of mental health (Rafferty, 2018). The use of culturally relevant expressive arts, such as dance (Bryant-Davis & Gobin, 2019; Lapp & Overmann, 2012) and music (Lapp & Overmann, 2012; Rafferty, 2018), was proposed as effective in engaging trafficking victims who identified as African American. Other creative strategies, such as sand tray or animal-assisted sessions, were also recommended (Lapp & Overmann, 2012).

### 6.5.1 *Cultural Humility*

To meet standards of best practices for working with multicultural populations, clinicians are encouraged to engage in a culturally humble manner (APA, 2017; Dewan, 2014; Waters & Asbill, 2013). *Cultural humility* encompasses an intentional and interpersonal attitude that seeks to understand cultural identity from the viewpoint of the other person. Waters and Asbill (2013) acknowledged three aspects that guide cultural humility: ongoing self-evaluation and self-critique, initiatives to rectify systemic power imbalances, and a development of advocacy-driven community connections. Cultural humility requires individuals to reject an all-knowing stance to flexibly and continually educate themselves on matters of diversity. It also entails a clinician's validation of an individual's own understanding of themselves and an active pursuit of accountability from systems that discriminate against multiracial and multiethnic individuals (Waters & Asbill, 2013). It is imperative that evaluators remain culturally humble and assess for presenting difficulties by utilizing various methodologies (e.g., conducting clinical observations, requesting self-report, administering culturally appropriate assessments, collecting collateral records and interviews) to avoid harm and re-traumatization of sex trafficking victims (APA, 2014; Ottisova et al., 2016).

### 6.5.2 *Risk Factors Impacting Multicultural Victims*

Multicultural individuals were exposed to a variety of risk factors that increased their likelihood of being trafficked for sex. The UNODC (2020) provided estimates of cases indicating preexisting factors that were taken advantage of by traffickers recruiting victims. Factors commonly impacting foreign nationals included economic need (51%); immigration status (10%); mental, behavioral, or neurological disorder (10%); and limited education or knowledge of foreign language (6%). Substance use (Baranowski, 2020; Cecchet & Thoburn, 2014; Cole & Sprang, 2015; Edinburgh et al., 2015) and sociocultural influencers on immigrant victims' viewpoints of mental disorders were also commonly present (Nsonwu, 2019; Rajan & Bryant-Davis, 2021). Moreover, high rates of feelings of guilt, employment difficulties, and language-based discrimination were perceived by Asian and Hispanic immigrants, with higher rates endorsed by the Asian immigrant groups (Li, 2016).

#### 6.5.2.1 Coercion Within Diverse Populations

Migration debt is a form of *debt bondage*, or bonded labor, that is frequently coerced by smugglers of persons (Sabon, 2018). Debt bondage refers to a trafficker's use of debt manipulation to coerce a person to engage in commercial sex (UNODC, 2020). Still, those smuggled into the United States are presumed to have consented to their migration and have repeatedly been perceived as violators of immigration regulations. Therefore, those who are sexually exploited in the process are at increased risk of being undetected as victims of sex trafficking (Lee, 2011; Sabon, 2018; UNODC, 2020).

Moreover, sociopolitical barriers of immigration policy influenced the manner in which individuals migrated into and within the United States. Smuggled migrants (i.e., persons whose illegal entry was facilitated by another individual for material benefit) reported giving up their valuable documents as collateral or becoming financially indebted to their smugglers (Dandurand, 2017; Lee, 2011; van Veldhuizen et al., 2017). This form of coercion recurrently precedes the exploitation of smuggled migrants for sex work upon their arrival. Fortunately, the DOJ and DHS continued developing efforts to improve transnational investigations of sex trafficking and convictions of traffickers (Dandurand, 2017; USDOS, 2021). Efforts included the agencies' collaborations with anti-trafficking authorities in Mexico and their operation of 13 Mexican state-level human trafficking task forces at the border between the United States and Mexico (USDOS, 2021). Nevertheless, migrants were not the only individuals exposed to sexual exploitation by means of debt bondage.

Reports in the United States described landlords forcing tenants in financial hardship to have sex with them to ward off homelessness (USDOS, 2021). Additionally, sex workers commonly entered financial relationships with traffickers unknowingly (Ottisova et al., 2016; Polaris, 2019). The routine exposure to economic transactions for sexual activities has made sex workers especially vulnerable to debts encompassing necessary expenses (e.g., food, housing, medical, transportation) and to the withholding of earnings controlled by their traffickers (Dandurand & Chin, 2014; Sisson, 2018; Polaris, 2019; UNODC, 2020).

LGTBQI+ youth were also found vulnerable to commercial sex as a result of their susceptibility to a multitude of hardships (e.g., experiences of poverty, histories of sexual abuse, and limited access to mental healthcare) and discrimination from community members or service providers (DeBoise, 2012; Naramore et al., 2017; UNODC, 2020). 20 transgender children and 133 transgender adults were identified as victims of trafficking by the DOJ between July 2016 and June 2017 (UNODC, 2018). Consequently, the overrepresentation of LGBTQI+ individuals among homeless youth in North America (estimated between 20% and 40%; UNODC, 2020) likely contributed to disparities in experiences of sex trafficking.

#### 6.5.2.2 Vulnerabilities Among Undocumented Victims

Threats of detainment and deportation greatly impact an immigrant's daily living and how they approach (or more so avoid) interactions with law enforcement personnel (Baranowski & Smith, 2018; Mann et al., 2014; Miller et al., 2018). Traffickers of persons controlled and extorted migrated victims with threats of exposure to authorities (UNODC, 2018, 2020). Fear-based expectations of contact with law enforcement have commonly provoked undocumented victims to experience persistent anticipation of separation from or endangerment of loved ones (Baranowski & Smith, 2018; Miller et al., 2018). In addition to events of threat, migrant victims of sex trafficking experienced numerous challenges that led to poor psychological outcomes, such as poverty, reduced occupational and academic opportunities (Li, 2016; Sisson, 2018), and limited access to mental health services or medical care (Garcini et al., 2020; Nsonwu, 2019).

Undocumented immigrants also endure distress due to restrictions relevant to their travel by plane or car (Baranowski & Smith, 2018; Garcini et al., 2017) and ineligibility to obtain a driver's license or other documentation (Baranowski & Smith, 2018; Mann et al., 2014). A link was observed between poorer psychological outcomes and undocumented legal status (Sangalang et al., 2019; Wylie et al., 2018) with an increase in the likelihood found for females (Cuevas et al., 2012; Kim et al., 2019; Murshid & Bowen, 2018). Increased psychological distress among immigration populations was most commonly seen across diagnostic contexts of anxiety, depression, and trauma-related symptomatology (Ahmed & Rasmussen, 2020; Garcini et al., 2017). Experiences of limited mobility options, loss of opportunities requiring valid forms of identification, and psychological impairment may all activate and prolong victim dependence on traffickers.

Oram et al. (2015) reported depression; PTSD, severe stress, and adjustment disorders; and schizophrenia and related disorders as the most prevalent diagnoses among men ($n$ = 18), women ($n$ = 78), and children ($n$ = 37) victims of sexual exploitation receiving mental health services in South London, UK. Adult victims originated from Europe (25%), Africa (48%), Asia (17%), and other countries (10%), whereas children arrived from Africa (54%), Asia (30%), and other countries (17%). Acute stress (38.7%), bipolar (30.2%), depersonalization (19.8%), dissociated identity (13.2%), and borderline personality (13.2%) disorders were also diagnosed among survivors. Specific difficulties relevant to mental health frequently endorsed by survivors comprised depression (88.7%), anxiety (76.4%), nightmares (73.6%), flashbacks (68.0%), low self-esteem (81.1%), and feelings of shame or guilt (82.1%) (Oram et al., 2015; Table 6.1).

### *6.5.3 Systemic Barriers to Multicultural Care*

Numerous systemic barriers exist between sex trafficking victims of multicultural backgrounds and the services offered by their surrounding community. Systemic barriers to the treatment of diverse populations include a lack of transcultural knowledge (APA, 2017; Albright et al., 2020; Dewan, 2014; Helton, 2016; Rajan & Bryant-Davis, 2021; Wylie et al., 2018), shortages of normative data across multicultural participants (Baranowski & Smith, 2018), clinician time constraints (Barber & Garcia, 2019; Wylie et al., 2018), and demonstration of judgment or discrimination at the time of service (Chavez-Dueñas et al., 2019; Haney et al., 2020). While sex trafficking victims were overall less likely to seek support and exit services, Dewan (2014) found that of foreign nationals trafficked to the United States, those

**Table 6.1** Risk factors and cultural considerations relevant to sex trafficking

| Risk factors | Population | Cultural considerations | Citation |
|---|---|---|---|
| Drug addiction<br>Illegal immigration status<br>Inadequate employment opportunities<br>Lack of education and knowledge of legal rights<br>Poverty | Internal (i.e., domestic) and external (i.e., transnational) | Cultural permissiveness of men having sex with minors (countries noted included Costa Rica, El Salvador, Guatemala, Honduras, Nicaragua, Panama, and the Dominican Republic)<br>Cultural traditions in migration<br>False promises of work abroad<br>Globalization and the rise of feminization in global markets<br>Machismo culture and the social tolerance of relevant practices<br>Patriarchal culture in Latin America | Zhang et al. (2012) |
| Decreased parental supervision and control<br>Domestic or intimate partner violence<br>Inner developmental struggle with independence, identity, sexuality, and relationships<br>Parental substance misuse<br>Widespread access to the Internet and advertising for sexual services | Domestic minor sex trafficking victims<br>Forensic nurses | Familial relationships with traffickers<br>Identification as a minority female of minor age | Sanchez and Pacquiao (2018) |
| Exposure to sex work<br>Extreme poverty, debt<br>Fraudulent work offers or travel for work<br>Negative expectations of law enforcement<br>Undocumented immigrant Latinas' lack of authorization to work in the United States | Victims detected by legal and social services (analysis of records)<br>Defense attorneys, prosecutor, and law enforcement officials (semi-structured interviews) | Immigrant victims were often coerced to claim legal status as a spouse, student, or tourist<br>Undocumented victims experienced a limitation of freedom due to visa and certification status and restrictions in obtaining relief<br>Perspectives of *snitching* and relevant consequences influenced underreporting among Latino victims<br>Undocumented migrants often faced smuggling debts<br>Transcultural victims appeared reluctant to participate in investigations due to their experiences of stigma and fear of legal rejection | Sabon (2018) |

(continued)

**Table 6.1** (continued)

| Risk factors | Population | Cultural considerations | Citation |
|---|---|---|---|
| Endorsement of substance abuse<br>History of state delinquency or dependency<br>Observed externalized behaviors (e.g., physical, emotional, or sexual aggression, truancy, vandalism)<br>Reported runaway behavior | Domestic minors that were sexually trafficked and involved in the child welfare system | Male and female youth in the welfare system appeared equally likely to affirm engagement in sex trafficking in the past 6 months<br>Male-identifying youth faced increased social pressures and shame related to their reporting of sexual exploitation | O'Brien et al. (2017) |
| High rates of adverse childhood experiences (ACEs)<br>Household dysfunction<br>Involvement in the juvenile justice system<br>Parental separation or divorce | 64,329 youth aged out of the juvenile justice system, including a group of youth involved in sex trafficking ($n$ = 102) | A disproportionate number of females and Black youth were arrested for trading sex compared to the overall population of offenders | Naramore et al. (2017) |
| Child victims of sexual exploitation were more likely to report histories of sexual abuse, failing grades, running away, and criminal conduct | A nation sample of 2598 state, county, and local law enforcement agencies were surveyed by mail<br>1051 investigators of specific child sexual exploitation cases were then interviewed by phone | Non-Hispanic Whites accounted for the majority of profiteers (56%) and purchasers (90%) detected, 5% of purchasers and 40% of profiteers identified as non-Hispanic Blacks<br>Profiteers were more likely to report prior arrests for sexual and nonsexual offenses, endorse a history of violence, involve more than one offender, and involve a female offender<br>Profiteer perpetrators of online sex trafficking were more likely to be women, younger than 40 years old, non-Hispanic Black, not a high school graduate, and less likely to be employed full time as compared to those making the illicit purchases<br>The majority of victims were female (82%) and between the ages of 13 and 17 (71%); 18% of victims detected lived in an urban community; 26% of cases involved offenders who were relatives of the victim | Mitchell et al. (2011) |

(continued)

**Table 6.1** (continued)

| Risk factors | Population | Cultural considerations | Citation |
|---|---|---|---|
| Exposure to racism<br>Minor age status<br>Racial identity of color | Minority youth of color | African American girls experienced physical and sexual abuse and sex trafficking at younger ages than their racial counterparts<br>Anti-trafficking laws appeared to target racial minorities through stigmatization and prosecution<br>Racial fetishes were found to provoke a demand for commercial sex with people of color | Butler (2015) |
| Migrant status | Court cases of human trafficking prosecuted in the United States between 2006 and 2011 that resulted in a conviction or plea bargain | Illegal migration to another country facilitated situations of human trafficking<br>Migrants were found to be both victims and perpetrators of sex trafficking | Denton (2016) |

from lower-tier countries of origin (i.e., countries whose governments do not comply with TVPA standards) indicated greater use of services. The author also reported that services relevant to mental health, social, and legal support were utilized most.

Several studies concluded that experiences of discrimination affect the mental health experiences of various immigrant (Monga et al., 2014; Rajan & Bryant-Davis, 2021) and non-immigrant (Albright et al., 2020; Buller et al., 2020; Gerassi, 2015; Sanchez & Pacquiao, 2018) victims of sex trafficking. Mann et al. (2014) addressed the long-standing stigma against individuals due to their immigration status albeit migrant contributions to the nation (Baranowski & Smith, 2018). Accounts of stigmatization against sex trafficking victims identifying as Black (APA, 2014; UNODC, 2021a; Brown, 2021; Butler, 2015; Pew Research Center, 2020), LGBTQ (UNODC, 2018, 2020, 2021b; DeBoise, 2012), or commercial sex workers (Dandurand, 2017; Farrell & Pfeffer, 2014; Naramore et al., 2017) were frequently recorded. Additionally, Vietnamese immigrants endorsed significant psychological distress associated with experiences of racial discrimination among (Kim et al., 2019), and a recent surge in hate crimes was observed against Asian individuals as a result of the COVID-19 pandemic (Asian Pacific Policy and Planning Council, 2020; Pew Research Center, 2020).

### 6.5.4 Cultural Challenges in Healthcare

The cultural differences between victims and authorized healthcare service providers also contribute to the underreporting of sex trafficking experiences to law enforcement agencies (APA, 2014; Dandurand & Chin, 2014; Dandurand, 2017; Farrell & Pfeffer, 2014; Haney et al., 2020; Sisson, 2018). Due to the overlap of identifying features existing within and across members of the foregoing diversity groups, those working with victims through best practices diligently identify intersectional facets contributing to victim identities and treatment experiences (APA, 2017).

Individuals who were sexually trafficked generally necessitated medical treatment for a variety of reasons (e.g., physical assault, sexual assault, sexual disease, general welfare examination), yet they were less likely to seek medical services (Nsonwu, 2019). The foregoing particularly extended to those undocumented, sexually trafficked, and in need of essential medical assistance (Garcini et al., 2020). Medical care options typically available to US citizens were not nearly as accessible to those who were undocumented (Garcini et al., 2020; Mann et al., 2014).

A prevalent resistance to seek necessary medical services is often observed among undocumented victims due to their inexperience with the US healthcare system, its costs, and formalities necessitated by care providers. Those who do seek medical care often resorted to emergency services (Dewan, 2014), which were typically associated with higher costs. Meanwhile, undocumented individuals living in the United States were found more likely to face healthcare challenges during the ongoing COVID-19 pandemic (Garcini et al., 2020; UNODC, 2020, 2021b; Vilches Hinojosa et al., 2021). A lack of accessibility to medical aid obstructs victims' paths to identification and intervention, given that healthcare professionals are instrumental in screening, identifying, and referring victims of sex trafficking for specialized care (Lederer & Wetzel, 2014; Gerassi et al., 2021; Helton, 2016).

Moreover, studies revealed a disproportionality in human immunodeficiency virus (HIV) exposure across immigrant populations from various countries (Levison et al., 2017; Mann et al., 2014; Sabri, 2018; Turner et al., 2021). Sabri (2018) reported that women who immigrated to the United States from African countries accounted for nearly 41% of HIV cases between California, Georgia, Washington State, Massachusetts, Minnesota, New Jersey, New York, and Virginia. Domestic victims of sex trafficking were overrepresented in HIV data as well, particularly within adult sex work (Bromfield, 2016; Turner et al., 2021) and youth (Le et al., 2018; Jaeckl & Laughon, 2021) populations. Turner and colleagues (2021) also provided evidence that the decriminalization of sex work and application of economic empowerment strategies could reduce HIV disparities in transwomen and other sex workers following their analysis of policies introduced in Congress to diminish sex trafficking.

Physical health symptoms most commonly endorsed among 105 American Indian and Alaskan Native, adult, female victims of sex trafficking included muscle pain (72%), impairments in memory or concentration (69% endorsed each), headaches (57%), vision problems (55%), stomach pain (48%), neck pain (44%), shortness of breath (39%), and nausea (36%) (Farley et al., 2016). Even though increased severity of physical symptoms correlated with greater endorsement of dissociation and PTSD (Farley et al., 2016) in victims, Native Americans were found more likely to seek help from a local traditional healer than a mental health professional (Bassett et al., 2014). Their choice in service provider may relate to the strong significance placed on dreams and spiritual practices by these individuals and serves as a protective factor against mental illness nevertheless (Bassett et al., 2014).

Given the complexity of healthcare demands among transcultural populations, it is imperative that a clinician practices cultural humility as they approach individuals in conversations about their private medical histories and potentially traumatic experiences surrounding the same. One must bear in mind that exposure to certain medical conditions, such as HIV (Levison et al., 2017) or TBI (Farley et al., 2016), may or may not occur in the context of a traumatic event involving sexual exploitation, and diagnoses of the medical sort may reciprocally activate or exacerbate post-traumatic stress (Levison et al., 2017). A transculturally competent clinician is not to shy away from addressing matters of diversity that impact victim welfare and treatment experiences.

### 6.5.5 Linguistic Implications

Language barriers were notable across all aspects of sex trafficking situations (Farrell & Pfeffer, 2014; Nsonwu, 2019), from victim recruitment to victim rescue. It is crucial that law enforcement officials and others providing responsive care be trained to credibly accommodate investigations involving linguistic barriers (i.e., use of interpreters, unbiased translators; APA, 2017; Baranowski, 2020). Unfortunately, the dismissal of linguistic-sensitive practices may lead to the corruption of a legitimate sex trafficking investigation. Cases have been cited in which patrol officers unknowingly utilized the trafficker to translate for a victim, facilitating the trafficker's ability to misrepresent the victim's testimony and evade detection of their criminally inhumane activities (Farrell & Pfeffer, 2014). Caution was also advised to clinicians explicitly diagnosing individuals through the use of orally translated interview and assessment questions (APA, 2017). Moreover, results of psychological testing were most effective when appropriate instruments were selected and provided in the examinee's intelligible language and adapted to represent the individual's cultural framework (Baranowski, 2020; Wylie et al., 2018).

#### 6.5.5.1 Diversity in Semantics and Relevant Clinical Presentations

In addition to diagnostic criteria, the DSM-5 provides context for (1) *cultural syndrome* (i.e., clusters of symptoms occurring in a specific cultural context); (2) *cultural idiom of distress* (i.e., common terms used to communicate distressing experiences), such as "kufungisisa" representing thought rumination among persons from Zimbabwe; and (3) *cultural explanation or perceived cause*, such as "maladi moun" in Haitian culture or "mal de ojo" in Hispanic regions (APA, 2013). A clinician's familiarity with cultural and somatic idioms may aid their understanding of multicultural victims' trauma-related symptoms. For example, study results indicated that PTSD criteria was most prevalent among women who narratively described experiences of severe *sustos* (Kimmell et al., 2020). Susto depicts a state of fear or fright, which could be underrated as a symptom of PTSD if one presumes the term to represent a surface-level concern. Therefore, an evaluator should not undermine the importance of semantics when presented with multicultural victim narratives that include cultural idioms.

*Ataques de nervios* (i.e., attack of nerves) is a cultural syndrome commonly seen among Latin and Hispanic populations. Ataques de nervios may entail aggressive or violent outbursts, resembling malice intent, upon an individual's experience of significant stress reaction (APA, 2013). By appreciating culturally influenced beliefs and behaviors, mental health professionals enhance therapeutic approaches suitable for victims in distress. After all, members of multicultural groups maintain individual standards of openness, communication, and general functioning (APA, 2017).

Victim perspectives on individualism and collectivism also impact their experience and disclosure of sex trafficking. Individualistic cultures place an emphasis on the individual, as opposed to collectivistic cultures, which center around group-based (e.g., familial, communal) values and needs (APA, 2017). Due to common collectivistic cultural expectations, such as males being perceived as strong, aggressive, and threating to demonstrate honor (Levison et al., 2017), collectivistically cultured victims were found susceptible to added pressures. The aforesaid aligns with the Latino notion of *Machismo*, which comprises Latin males as the protectors of their communities and encourages them to develop a robust masculinity (Zhang et al., 2012). One may consider machismo as a presenting feature across both Latino male victims, who underreport their experiences of sexual exploitation (Levison et al., 2017; Mann et al., 2014), and Latino male traffickers, who assert their dominance over their victims (Sabon, 2018; Zhang et al., 2012).

## 6.6 Multicultural Experiences of Trauma

A traumatic event is defined by the DSM-5 as an exposure to actual or threatened death, serious injury, or sexual violence by way of experiencing the event, witnessing the event occurring to others, learning of the event happening to a close relative or friend, or repeatedly being exposed to aversive details of events (APA, 2013). The

DSM-5 description of a traumatic event is disputed by mental health experts due to its omission of additional traumatic aspects relevant to distress and impairment in functioning, such as poverty, emotional abuse, and unjust or prejudicial treatment (Ballard-Kang, 2020). As mentioned earlier in this chapter, the foregoing aspects overlap with risks and barriers commonly encountered by victims of sex trafficking.

Sexual exploitation, assault, and abuse are each considered to be a potentially traumatic event (PTE) and relate to the trafficking of humans for sex. A PTE comprises any event that may activate the development of posttraumatic stress disorder (PTSD, i.e., exposure to actual or threatened death, serious injury, or sexual violence, American Psychiatric Association [APA], 2013). PTEs may occur interpersonally, repeatedly, or prolongedly; thus, they impose lasting consequences on those who experience them. PTEs frequently catalyze an individual's migration and increase their vulnerability to further maltreatment (Ahmed & Rasmussen, 2020), including experiences of sex trafficking (Hershberger, 2021; Hossain et al., 2010).

Victims of certain diverse backgrounds endorsed increased threat of experiencing particular distressing events. For example, PTEs of a sexually violent nature were regularly reported by immigrant (Barber & Garcia, 2019; Cuevas et al., 2012; Kim et al., 2019; Sangalang et al., 2019), Black (UNODC, 2021a; Brown, 2021; Butler, 2015), LGBTQ (2020 Report; UNODC, 2021a, Polaris, 2019), and sex work (APA, 2014; DeBoise, 2014; Gerassi, 2015) populations at alarming rates (APA, 2014; DeBoise, 2014; Gerassi, 2015).

Nevertheless, not all victims of PTEs exhibit distress or impairment in response to their exploitation, particularly those with resilient features (APA, 2017; Baranowski, 2020; Cecchet & Thoburn, 2014; Ford-Paz et al., 2020). Protective factors reported to increase resilience in sex trafficking survivors included religious or spiritual orientation (Ottisova et al., 2016), social support (Cecchet & Thoburn, 2014; Gerassi et al., 2021), and access to legal relief (Kim et al., 2019; Oram et al., 2015; Sabon, 2018).

### 6.6.1 Potentially Traumatic Events and Victim Populations

Migrant Latino females reported high rates of *polyvictimization*, meaning that their victimization was often prolonged, occurred multiple times, and frequently resulted in complex trauma (Cuevas et al., 2012). Victims who were trafficked into the United States endorsed pre- and post-migration trauma-related experiences (Cuevas et al., 2012; Kim et al., 2019). Pre-migration traumas are those that are experienced prior to departing from a country or region of origin, whereas post-migration traumas are those experienced in the host location. Likewise, survivors of sex trafficking experience traumatic events both prior to and during trafficking (Hossain et al., 2010). Examples of PTEs commonly reported by US immigrants include gang violence, sexual assault (Barber & Garcia, 2019), war, torture, poverty, natural disasters (Ahmed & Rasmussen, 2020), kidnapping, and exposure to violent deaths (Li,

2016). Trauma reported during migration included human trafficking (Garcini et al., 2017), torture, and sexual assault (Miller et al., 2018).

Albeit federal legislation enforced to protect foreign national victims vulnerable to complex trauma (UNODC, 2021a), Asian (i.e., Chinese, Filipino, Vietnamese, other Asian) and Latino (i.e., Cuban, Puerto Rican, Mexican, other Hispanic) immigrants, who endorsed pre-migration trauma exposure, were at higher risk of experiencing another traumatic event after migrating to the United States compared to those who denied exposure to pre-migration trauma (Li, 2016). Relatedly, post-migration trauma was associated with greater psychological distress among refugees and with depressive disorders and psychological distress among non-refugee immigrants (Sangalang et al., 2019). Similar to immigrant women from African countries (Sabri, 2018), Vietnamese refugees disclosed multiple traumatic experiences and endorsed psychological distress due to trauma exposure both pre- and post-migration (Kim et al., 2019). Victims also experienced trauma events on their routes to host destinations, post-migration trauma symptoms appeared immediately or delayed, and symptoms were deemed capable of worsening over time (Ballard-Kang, 2020).

A study of 105 adult, female, American Indian, and Alaskan Native victims of sex trafficking revealed participants reported experiencing homelessness (98%), threats with a weapon (78%), physical assault (84%), rape (92%), repeated rape (i.e., five times or more, 68%), childhood physical assault by a caregiver (56%), childhood sexual abuse (79%), and traumatic brain injury (TBI) as a result of violence (Farley et al., 2016). While high levels of violence were reported by sex trafficking victims within the United States (Cecchet & Thoburn, 2014; Hopper & Gonzalez, 2018), international victims disclosed similar experiences (Hossain et al., 2010; Kiss et al., 2015). Of 204 European minor and adult females interviewed post-trafficking, over 80% reported sexual violence, threats of harm to themselves, and persistently restricted freedom experienced during trafficking (Hossain et al., 2010). With respect to pre-trafficking trauma experiences, 15% endorsed child sexual abuse, and 25% endorsed sexual violence in adulthood. Survivors originated from Belgium (1.5%), Bulgaria (9.8%), Czech Republic (2.5%), Italy (12.7%), Moldova (36.3%), Ukraine (24.5%), and the United Kingdom (12.7%).

Furthermore, exposures to racism or ethno-violence place minority individuals at higher risk of perceiving a threat against their well-being, particularly when accompanied by PTEs (Chavez-Dueñas et al., 2019). Increased exposure to discrimination also correlated with increased likelihood of meeting criteria for a mental health diagnosis (Garcini et al., 2017). Meanwhile, victims are prone to re-traumatization following their experience of sexual exploitation (APA, 2014); thus, it is recommended that a trauma-informed approach be implemented when communicating with survivors of sex trafficking (APA, 2014; Hershberger, 2021; Johnson, 2020; Powell et al., 2017).

### 6.6.2 Trauma-Informed Care of Diverse Victims in the United States

The complex nature of victim presentations elicits service providers' use of trauma-informed, evidence-based strategies and encourages cultivation of culturally sensitive knowledge (Hershberger, 2021; Office to Monitor and Combat Trafficking in Persons, 2021; Rajan & Bryant-Davis, 2021). The application of such practices facilitates victim disclosure (Gerassi et al., 2021), fosters therapeutic progress (Hershberger, 2021; Powell et al., 2017), and safeguards the clinician's ethical duty of avoiding harm (APA, 2017; Office to Monitor and Combat Trafficking in Persons, 2021). Clinical forensic evaluation skills are valuable for assessing victim qualifications of criteria required for relief or to guide those involved in the victim's integrative care (including the victim; Barber & Garcia, 2019; Murshid & Bowen, 2018). Yet, despite honest efforts made by mental health service providers, challenges and inconsistencies were observed across professional practice of transcultural, trauma-informed care (Helton, 2016; Lederer & Wetzel, 2014; Murshid & Bowen, 2018; Wylie et al., 2018).

The Office to Monitor and Combat Trafficking in Persons (2021) recommended the implementation of an integration process to establish a trauma-informed workplace and empower survivors of human trafficking. Ideas spanned from the modeling of best practices relevant to self-care by providers to the employment of survivors for leadership positions in victim care. Powell et al. (2017) noted positive treatment outcomes for victims of human trafficking who were approached in a client-centered manner by clinicians who sought trauma-informed training. Individual therapy, group counseling, trauma-focused cognitive behavioral therapy (TFCBT) (Johnson, 2020; Lapp & Overmann, 2012; Rafferty, 2018), eye movement desensitization and reprocessing (EMDR), and family therapy were all proposed as treatment modalities for addressing trauma with sex trafficking victims as well (Lapp & Overmann, 2012). Those providing brief interventions should consider maintaining an easily accessible list of multicultural referral contacts (e.g., therapists with bilingual abilities, legal aid, trauma-informed medical providers, sources for welfare services) for when a victim necessitates them.

In 2018, the DOJ devoted \$1.2 million toward efforts to increase the use of trauma-informed services to support victims of human trafficking (UNODC, 2021a). Furthermore, \$31.2 million in funds was provided to 45 service providers who offered comprehensive services to victim in the United States (UNODC, 2021a). The budget for specialized care was increased significantly, considering that nearly half (i.e., \$16.2 million) was contributed in 2017, which demonstrated systemic efforts put forth by members of the US government to improve victim response. A professional approaching a multicultural victim through a trauma-informed viewpoint would acknowledge whether any prevailing barriers are present and the extent to which they impact the individual's treatment experiences (Albright et al., 2020; Powell et al., 2017; Rafferty, 2018) (Table 6.2).

**Table 6.2** Recommendations for trauma-informed care of sex trafficking victims

| Trauma | Clinical purpose | Recommendations for care | Citation |
|---|---|---|---|
| Potentially traumatic migration journeys<br>Torture<br>War | Assessment of mental health services provided to immigrants and refugees in London, Ontario | Use of a family-based approach to address intergenerational or complex trauma<br>Application of flexible, person-centered methods<br>Standardization of assessments for immigrants and refugees<br>Improvement of training in trauma and transculturally informed models of care<br>Use of assessments with an interpreter present | Wylie et al. (2018) |
| Sexual exploitation<br>Violence | Examine social determinants of victim vulnerability<br>Improve prevention and care | Develop interprofessional platforms to address local and state policies<br>Collaborate with interdisciplinary team members (e.g., forensic nurses, educators, agencies<br>Utilize trauma-informed methods to assess a victim's developmental level and provide skills building practices (e.g., self-esteem, interpersonal, education, occupation)<br>Implement the ecological model and person-centered approaches | Sanchez and Pacquiao (2018) |
| Human trafficking | Encourage the employment of experts with lived experience of human trafficking to aid in anti-trafficking efforts | Aim for a survivor-informed approach through hiring survivors as staff members and implementing their recommendations and feedback into practice<br>Encourage diverse self-care practices as part of the organizational culture | Office to Monitor and Combat Trafficking in Persons (2021) |

(continued)

**Table 6.2** (continued)

| Trauma | Clinical purpose | Recommendations for care | Citation |
|---|---|---|---|
| Human trafficking<br>Intimate partner violence<br>Sexual assault | Analyze the Violence Against Women Act (VAWA) from a trauma-informed viewpoint | Aim to prevent re-traumatization<br>Empower immigrants to use services and advocate for their rights<br>Prioritize trustworthiness and transparency<br>Promote collaboration between victims, service providers, and community members<br>Recognize the intersectional identities of victims<br>Understand policy impacting victims (e.g., visa participants not being required to assist authorities if they are at further risk of harm) and provide relevant psychoeducation | Murshid and Bowen (2018) |
| Self-harm behaviors (e.g., cutting, suicide attempts)<br>Sexual abuse of younger peers by older girls in victim aftercare facility<br>Violent behavior and sexual abuse by staff members or law enforcement personnel | Improve mental health services for victims<br>Provide culturally appropriate, trauma-informed alternatives to traditional therapy or other comprehensive services | Acknowledge each victim's hierarchy of needs<br>Be cautious of cultural viewpoints relevant to care (e.g., Vietnamese preference for "healing practices" over "therapy")<br>Consider physical impacts of trauma on the body (e.g., somatic symptoms, physiological symptoms)<br>Encourage engagement in additional therapeutic activities (e.g., massage, acupuncture, meditation, gardening, yoga, dance)<br>Identify financial and human resources or seek comprehensive case management<br>Use mental health assessments to guide treatment | Rafferty (2018) |

(continued)

**Table 6.2** (continued)

| Trauma | Clinical purpose | Recommendations for care | Citation |
|---|---|---|---|
| Abused by a person of authority (50.5%)<br>Beaten (68.9%)<br>Forced sex (81.6%)<br>Forced sex recorded for pornographic purposes (17.1%)<br>Strangled (54.4%)<br>Threatened with a weapon (66.0%) | Identify health consequences endorsed across focus groups of 107 domestic victims of sex trafficking ranging between ages 14 and 60 | Attend to signs of physical and sexual exploitation (e.g., signs of forced sex, bodily bruises, head or facial injuries, multiple sexual diseases and infections)<br>Seek multicultural training in identifying and treating possible trafficking victims<br>Maintain internal protocols, procedures, and regulations to ensure one-on-one communications between the service provider and potential victim (e.g., a private interview, separation for paperwork)<br>Schedule time for more than one visit<br>Use informal language, including slang, rather than formal or clinical terms<br>Victims were more likely to return if they were advised that a healthcare issue needed to be reevaluated | Lederer and Wetzel (2014) |
| Family violence<br>Intimate partner violence<br>Sex trafficking | African American girls and women exiting sex trafficking | Implement culturally contextualized narrative therapy within support groups of participants with similar racial identities<br>Recognize the potential impacts of oppression, intergenerational trauma, and race-based traumatic stress<br>Provide cognitive behavioral trauma-focused treatment with integrated exposure techniques and mindfulness-based stress reduction | Rajan and Bryant-Davis (2021) |

## 6.7 Conclusion

Several risk factors (e.g., undocumented immigration status, financial hardship, limited education, restricted knowledge of language) increased multicultural victims' exposure to sex trafficking. Moreover, individuals migrating into the United States were found susceptible to ignorance, fraud, and deception due to their unfamiliarity with policies and social welfare systems (e.g., healthcare, food assistance, housing subsidies, education, childcare, legal aid). Nevertheless, it is imperative to acknowledge the strengths and limitations of existing data on the cultural diversity of sex trafficking victims and perpetrators. A lack of empirical studies on sex trafficking (Okech et al., 2018) was expected, given the nature of trafficking and difficulties in obtaining accurate data.

The availability of public data on identified sex trafficking victims and relevant statistics depends on a range of factors. For instance, agencies and organizations may collect data that is not organized or disseminated for researchers or community audiences to access. Data that is published is not always gathered consistently or presented as all-inclusive. Notably, diversity is not exclusively addressed by solely distinguishing one's gender, race, and age, as most commonly recorded in studies. Additional aspects of an examinee's identity, such as their ethnicity, religion, spiritual beliefs, immigration status, LGBTQ+, and socioeconomic and disability demographics, are to be investigated.

When acknowledging cultural factors relevant to patterns of sex trafficking, service providers must consider not only the victims but also their communities. Acculturative experiences are of particular importance in the development of appropriate recommendations for foreign national victims of sex trafficking. Additionally, language and cultural barriers often limit a foreign national victim's ability to recognize their rights, trust service providers, report their traffickers, and request supports. Meanwhile, socioeconomic barriers that increased immigrant vulnerability and exposure to situations of exploitation for commercial sex simultaneously deterred criminal reports against sex traffickers and identification of undocumented victims in need. Therefore, service providers must make efforts to not only evaluate barriers to ethical treatment of detected victims but to also thoroughly screen potential victims when opportunities to provide medical care or legal assistance arise.

Since victims who emigrate into the United States originate from various destinations, it is wise of those practicing in response or care settings to seek training as to how they may adapt their assessments, impressions, and treatment recommendations to individuals from diverse origins. Additional emphasis is to be placed on adapting traditional Western intervention practices to address cultural variations across sex trafficking victim populations. It is also recommended that those working with victims actively aim to destigmatize victim experiences. Healthcare and law enforcement responders may improve victim identification and care through authentically practicing cultural sensitivity, addressing social inequalities, and working through skill development opportunities with victims in a trauma-informed manner.

Since coercive methods used by traffickers comprise a broad array of exploitative means, such as physical injury, psychosocial or reputational harms, threats of danger to others, and financial manipulation, victims endorse a variety of mental health and medical issues. A clinician's knowledge of the individual and systemic opportunities available and accessible to multicultural victims facilitates a greater understanding of victim experience and reinforces victim advocacy efforts. The foregoing is currently of particular relevance given that transnational relations are reinforced by the Internet and global markets. Meanwhile, amplified hardships were recently experienced worldwide as governments executed pandemic-related efforts baring impact on anti-trafficking policies and patterns of travel and thus on trends of human trafficking.

## References


Ahmed, S., & Rasmussen, A. (2020). Changes in social status and postmigration mental health among west African immigrants. *American Journal of Orthopsychiatry, 90*(2), 171–180. https://doi-org.ezproxylocal.library.nova.edu/10.1037/ort0000419

American Psychiatric Association. (2013). *Diagnostic and statistical manual of mental disorders* (5th ed.). Publisher.

American Psychological Association. (2014). *Report of the task force on trafficking of women and girls.* https://www.apa.org/pi/women/programs/trafficking/report.pdf

American Psychological Association. (2017). *Multicultural Guidelines: An Ecological Approach to Context, Identity, and Intersectionality.* Retrieved from: http://www.apa.org/about/policy/multicultural-guidelines.pdf

American Psychological Association. (2020). *APA Dictionary of Psychology.*

Albright, K., Greenbaum, J., Edwards, S. A., & Tsai, C. (2020, February). Systematic review of facilitators of, barriers to, and recommendations for healthcare services for child survivors of human trafficking globally. *Child Abuse & Neglect, 100.*

Asian Pacific Policy and Planning Council. (2020). *Stop AAPI hate.* https://www.asianpacificpolicyandplanningcouncil.org/stop-aapi-hate/

Ballard-Kang, J. L. (2020). Using culturally appropriate, trauma-informed support to promote bicultural self-efficacy among resettled refugees: A conceptual model. *Journal of Ethnic & Cultural Diversity in Social Work, 1–3*, 23. https://doi.org/10.1080/15313204.2017.1409676

Baranowski, K. A. (2020). Documenting human rights violations: An introduction to the psychological evaluation of asylum seekers. *Practice Innovations, 5*(1), 32–44. http://dx.doi.org.ezproxylocal.library.nova.edu/10.1037/pri0000105

Baranowski, K. A., & Smith, L. (2018). Working with undocumented immigrants from Mexico: Experiences of practitioners in New Mexico and Texas. *Professional Psychology: Research & Practice, 49*(3), 185–192. https://doi-org.ezproxylocal.library.nova.edu/10.1037/pro0000191

Barber, R. V., & Garcia, M. A. (2019). Special considerations when conducting forensic psychological evaluations for immigration court. *Journal of Clinical Psychology, 11*, 2049. https://doi.org/10.1002/jclp.22863

Bassett, D., Buchwald, D., & Manson, S. (2014). Posttraumatic stress disorder and symptoms among American Indians and Alaska Natives: A review of the literature. *Social Psychiatry and Psychiatric Epidemiology, 49*(3), 417–433. https://doi.org/10.1007/s00127-013-0759-y

Batalova, J., Blizzard, B., & Bolter, J. (2020). Frequently requested statistics on immigrants and immigration in the United States. *Migration Policy Institute.* https://www.migrationpolicy.org/article/frequentlyrequested-statistics-immigrants-and-immigration-united-states.

Bromfield, N. F. (2016). Sex slavery and sex trafficking of women in the United States: Historical and contemporary parallels, policies, and perspectives in social work. *Affilia: Journal of Women & Social Work, 31*(1), 129–139. https://doi-org.ezproxylocal.library.nova.edu/10.1177/0886109915616437

Brown, P. J. (2021, March 22). Disparate impact considerations in human trafficking cases. *Judges Journal, 60*(2), 8. https://search-ebscohost-com.ezproxylocal.library.nova.edu/login.aspx?direct=true&db=edsgao&AN=edsgcl.660730528&site=eds-live

Bryant-Davis, T., & Gobin, R. L. (2019). Still we rise: Psychotherapy for African American girls and women exiting sex trafficking. *Women & Therapy, 42*(3–4), 385–405. https://www.tandfonline.com/doi/abs/10.1080/02703149.2019.1622902

Budiman, A., Tamir, C., Mora, L., & Noe-Bustamante, L. (2020). *Facts on United States immigrants, 2018: Statistical portrait of the foreign-born population in the United States*. Pew Research Center. Retrieved August 28, 2020, from https://www.pewresearch.org/hispanic/2020/08/20/facts-on-u-s-immigrants/

Buller, A. M., Pichon, M., McAlpine, A., Cislaghi, B., Heise, L., et al. (2020, June). Systematic review of social norms, attitudes, and factual beliefs linked to the sexual exploitation of children and adolescents. *Child Abuse & Neglect, 104*.

Butler, C. N. (2015). The racial roots of human trafficking. *UCLA Law Review, 62*, 1464.

Cecchet, S. J., & Thoburn, J. (2014). The psychological experience of child and adolescent sex trafficking in the United States: Trauma and resilience in survivors. *Psychological Trauma: Theory, Research, Practice, and Policy, 6*(5), 482–493. https://doi.org/10.1037/a0035763

Chavez-Dueñas, N. Y., Adames, H. Y., Perez-Chavez, J. G., & Salas, S. P. (2019). Healing ethno-racial trauma in Latinx immigrant communities: Cultivating hope, resistance, and action. *American Psychologist, 74*(1), 49. https://doi.org/10.1037/amp0000289

Chen, W. Y. (2010). Exposure to community violence and adolescents' internalizing behaviors among African American and Asian American adolescents. *Journal of Youth and Adolescence, 39*(4), 403–413. https://doi-org.ezproxylocal.library.nova.edu/10.1007/s10964-009-9427-7

Cole, J., & Sprang, G. (2015). Sex trafficking of minors in metropolitan, micropolitan, and rural communities. *Child Abuse & Neglect, 40*, 113–123. https://doi.org/10.1016/j.chiabu.2014.07.015

Cuevas, C. A., Sabina, C., & Bell, K. A. (2012). The effect of acculturation and immigration on the victimization and psychological distress link in a national sample of Latino women. *Journal of Interpersonal Violence, 27*(8), 1428. https://doi.org/10.1177/0886260511425797

Dandurand, Y. (2017). Human trafficking and police governance. *Police Practice & Research, 18*(3), 322–336. https://doi-org.ezproxylocal.library.nova.edu/10.1080/15614263.2017.1291599

Dandurand, Y., & Chin, V. (2014). Implementation of transnational criminal law: Issues and challenges. In *Routledge handbook of transnational criminal law* (pp. 461–476).

DeBoise, C. (2012, January 11). *Human trafficking of immigrant transgender women: Hidden in the shadows* [Blog post]. Retrieved from http://www.race-talk.org/human-trafficking-of-immigrant-transgender-women-hidden-in-the-shadows/

DeBoise, C. (2014). Human trafficking and sex work: Foundational social-work principles. *Meridians, 12*(1), 227–233. https://doi.org/10.2979/meridians.12.1.227

Denton, E. (2016). Anatomy of offending: Human trafficking in the United States, 2006–2011. *Journal of Human Trafficking, 2*(1), 32–62.

Dewan, S. (2014). Patterns of service utilization among pre-certified victims of human trafficking. *International Social Work, 57*(1), 64–74. https://doi.org/10.1177/0020872813507592

Edinburgh, L., Pape-Blabolil, J., Harpin, S. B., & Saewyc, E. (2015, August). Assessing exploitation experiences of girls and boys seen at a Child Advocacy Center. *Child Abuse & Neglect, 46*, 47–59.

Farley, M., Deer, S., Golding, J., Matthews, N., Lopez, G., Stark, C., & Hudon, E. (2016). The prostitution and trafficking of American Indian/Alaska Native women in Minnesota. *American Indian and Alaska Native Mental Health Research, 23*(1), 65–104. https://doi.org/10.5820/aian.2301.2016.65

Farrell, A., & Pfeffer, R. (2014). Policing human trafficking: Cultural blinders and organizational barriers. *Annals of the American Academy of Political and Social Science, 653*, 46–64. http://heinonline.org.ezproxylocal.library.nova.edu/HOL/Page?handle=hein.cow/anamacp0653&div=4

Federal Bureau of Investigations. (n.d.). *Civil rights*. https://www.fbi.gov/investigate/civil-rights

Federal Bureau of Investigations. (2021, September). *Crime data explorer: Human trafficking*. https://crime-data-explorer.app.cloud.gov/#.

Fedina, L., Williamson, C., & Perdue, T. (2019). Risk factors for domestic child sex trafficking in the United States. *Journal of Interpersonal Violence, 34*(13), 2653–2673. https://doi-org.ezproxylocal.library.nova.edu/10.1177/0886260516662306

Ford-Paz, R. E., Santiago, C. D., Coyne, C. A., Rivera, C., Guo, S., Rusch, D., St Jean, N., Hilado, A., & Cicchetti, C. (2020). You're not alone: A public health response to immigrant/refugee distress in the current sociopolitical context. *Psychological Services, 17*, 128–138. https://doi--org.ezproxylocal.library.nova.edu/10.1037/ser0000381

Garcini, L. M., Peña, J. M., Galvan, T., Fagundes, C. P., Malcarne, V., el al. (2017). Mental Disorders Among Undocumented Mexican Immigrants in High-Risk Neighborhoods: Prevalence, Comorbidity, and Vulnerabilities. *Journal of Consulting and Clinical Psychology, 10*, 927. DOI:10.1037/ccp0000237

Garcini, L. M., Domenech Rodríguez, M. M., Mercado, A., & Paris, M. (2020). A Tale of Two Crises: The Compounded Effect of COVID-19 and Anti-Immigration Policy in the United States. *Psychological Trauma: Theory, Research, Practice & Policy, 12*, S230–S232. https://doi.org/10.1037/tra0000775

Gerassi, L. (2015, August). From exploitation to industry: Definitions, risks, and consequences of domestic sexual exploitation and sex work among women and girls. *Journal of Human Behavior in the Social Environment, 25*(6), 591–605.

Gerassi, L., Edmond, T. E., Fabbre, V., Howard, A., & Nichols, A. J. (2021). Disclosing sex trading histories to providers: Barriers and facilitators to navigation of social services among women impacted by commercial sexual exploitation. *Journal of Interpersonal Violence, 36*(3-4), NP1259–1284NP.

Haney, K., LeBeau, K., Bodner, S., Czizik, A., Young, M. E., et al. (2020). Sex trafficking in the United States: A scoping review. *Journal of Evidence-Based Social Work, 17*(6), 714–748.

Helton, M. (2016). Human trafficking: How a joint task force between health care providers and law enforcement can assist with identifying victims and prosecuting traffickers. *Health Matrix: Journal of Law-Medicine, 26*, 433–xiv. http://heinonline.org.ezproxylocal.library.nova.edu/HOL/Page?handle=hein.journals/hmax26&div=16

Hershberger, J. M. (2021). A relational-cultural theory approach to work with survivors of sex trafficking. *Journal of Creativity in Mental Health, 16*(4), 456–466. https://doi-org.ezproxylocal.library.nova.edu/10.1080/15401383.2020.1790457

Hopper, E. K., & Gonzalez, L. D. (2018). A comparison of psychological symptoms in survivors of sex and labor trafficking. *Behavioral Medicine, 44*(3), 177–188. https://doi.org/10.1080/08964289.2018.1432551

Hossain, M., Zimmerman, C., Abas, M., Light, M., & Watts, C. (2010). The relationship of trauma to mental disorders among trafficked and sexually exploited girls and women. *American Journal of Public Health, 100*(12), 2442–2449. https://doi.org/10.2105/AJPH.2009.173229

Hwang, W.-C. (2021, January 1). Demystifying and addressing internalized racism and oppression among Asian Americans. *American Psychologist, 76*(4), 596–610. http://explore.bl.uk/primo_library/libweb/action/display.do?tabs=detailsTab&gathStatTab=true&ct=display&fn=search&doc=ETOCRN627453620&indx=1&recIds=ETOCRN627453620

Jaeckl, S., & Laughon, K. (2021). Risk factors and indicators for commercial sexual exploitation/domestic minor sex trafficking of adolescent girls in the United States in the context of school nursing: An integrative review of the literature. *Journal of School Nursing, 37*(1), 6–16. https://doi-org.ezproxylocal.library.nova.edu/10.1177/1059840520971806

Johnson, B. C. (2020). Featured counter-trafficking program: Trauma recovery for victims of sex trafficking. *Child Abuse & Neglect*, 100. https://doi-org.ezproxylocal.library.nova.edu/10.1016/j.chiabu.2019.104153

Kim, I., Keovisai, M., Kim, W., Richards-Desai, S., & Yalim, A. C. (2019). Trauma, discrimination, and psychological distress across vietnamese refugees and immigrants: A life course perspective. *Community Mental Health Journal, 55*(3), 385–393. https://doi-org.ezproxylocal.library.nova.edu/10.1007/s10597-018-0268-2

Kimmell, J., Mendenhall, E., & Jacobs, E. A. (2020). Deconstructing PTSD: Trauma and emotion among Mexican immigrant women. *Transcultural Psychiatry, 1363461520903120*. https://doi.org/10.1177/1363461520903120

Kiss, L., Pocock, N. S., Naisanguansri, V., Suos, S., Dickson, B., Thuy, D., Koehler, J., Sirisup, K., Pongrungsee, N., Nguyen, V. A., Borland, R., Dhavan, P., & Zimmerman, C. (2015). Health of men, women, and children in post-trafficking services in Cambodia, Thailand, and Vietnam: An observational cross-sectional study. *The Lancet Global Health, 3*, 154–161. https://doi.org/10.1016/S2214-109X(15)70016-1

Lapp, C. A., & Overmann, N. (2012). Mental health perspectives on the care of human trafficking victims within our borders. In *Sex trafficking: A clinical guide for nurses* (Vol. 305).

Lauger, A. D., & Durose, M. R. (2021). *Human trafficking data collection activities, 2021*. https://calio.dspacedirect.org/handle/11212/5261

Le, P. D., Ryan, N., Rosenstock, Y., & Goldmann, E. (2018). Health issues associated with commercial sexual exploitation and sex trafficking of children in the United States: A systematic review. *Behavioral Medicine, 44*(3), 219–233. https://doi-org.ezproxylocal.library.nova.edu/10.1080/08964289.2018.1432554

Lee, M. aut. (2011). *Trafficking and global crime control*. Maggy Lee. http://swbplus.bsz-bw.de/bsz318964368kla.htm

Lederer, L. J., & Wetzel, C. A. (2014). The health consequences of sex trafficking and their implications for identifying victims in healthcare facilities. *Annals of Health Law, 23*, 61.

Levison, J. H., Bogart, L. M., Khan, I. F., Mejia, D., Amaro, H., Alegría, M., & Safren, S. (2017). "Where It Falls Apart": Barriers to retention in HIV care in Latino immigrants and migrants. *AIDS Patient Care and STDs, 31*(9), 394–405. https://doi-org.ezproxylocal.library.nova.edu/10.1089/apc.2017.0084

Li, M. (2016). Pre-migration trauma and post-migration stressors for Asian and Latino American immigrants: Transnational stress proliferation. *Social Indicators Research, 129*(1), 47–59. https://doi.org/10.1007/s11205-015-1090-7

Mann, L., Valera, E., Hightow-Weidman, L. B., & Barrington, C. (2014). Migration and HIV risk: Life histories of Mexican-born men living with HIV in North Carolina. *Culture, Health & Sexuality, 16*(7–8), 820–834. https://doi.org/10.1080/13691058.2014.918282

Miller, A., Bybee, D., Goodkind, J. R., & Hess, J. M. (2018). Understanding the mental health consequences of family separation for refugees: Implications for policy and practice. *American Journal of Orthopsychiatry, 88*(1), 26. https://doi.org/10.1037/ort0000272

Mitchell, K. J., Jones, L. M., Finkelhor, D., & Wolak, J. (2011, March). Internet-facilitated commercial sexual exploitation of children: Findings from a nationally representative sample of law enforcement agencies in the United States. *Sexual Abuse: Journal of Research and Treatment, 23*(1), 43–71.

Monga, P., Keller, A., & Venters, H. (2014). Prevention and punishment: Barriers to accessing health services for undocumented immigrants in the United States. *Laws, 3*(1), 50–60.

Murshid, N. S., & Bowen, E. A. (2018). A trauma-informed analysis of the violence against women act's provisions for undocumented immigrant women. *Violence Against Women, 24*(13), 1540–1556. https://doi-org.ezproxylocal.library.nova.edu/10.1177/1077801217741991

Naramore, R., Bright, M. A., Epps, N., & Hardt, N. S. (2017, June). Youth arrested for trading sex have the highest rates of childhood adversity: A statewide study of juvenile offenders. *Sexual Abuse: Journal of Research and Treatment, 29*(4), 396–410.

National Human Trafficking Hotline. (2020, December). *2020 National Hotline Annual Report*. https://humantraffickinghotline.org/resources/2020-national-hotline-annual-report\.

Nsonwu, M. (2019, January 1). Human trafficking of immigrants and refugees in North Carolina. *North Carolina Medical Journal, 80*(2), 101–103. http://explore.bl.uk/primo_library/libweb/action/display.do?tabs=detailsTab&gathStatTab=true&ct=display&fn=search&doc=ETOCRN619419687&indx=1&recIds=ETOCRN619419687

O'Brien, J. E., White, K., & Rizo, C. F. (2017). Domestic minor sex trafficking among child welfare–involved youth: An exploratory study of correlates. *Child Maltreatment, 22*(3), 265–274. https://doi.org/10.1177/1077559517709995

Office to Monitor and Combat Trafficking in Persons. (2021, July 1). *Unifying trauma-informed practices and voices of survivor leadership* [Fact sheet]. United States Department of State. https://www.state.gov/unifying-trauma-informed-practices-and-voices-of-survivorleadership/#:~:text=According%20to%20the%20U.S.%20Substance,approach%20into%20the%20creation%20of

Okech, D., Choi, Y. J., Elkins, J., & Burns, A. C. (2018). Seventeen years of human trafficking research in social work: A review of the literature. *Journal of Evidence-Informed Social Work, 15*(2), 103–122.

Oram, S., Khondoker, M., Abas, M., Broadbent, M., & Howard, L. M. (2015). Characteristics of trafficked adults and children with severe mental illness: A historical cohort study. *Lancet Psychiatry, 2*, 1084–1091.

Ottisova, L., Hemmings, S., Howard, L. M., Zimmerman, C., & Oram, S. (2016, August). Prevalence and risk of violence and the mental, physical and sexual health problems associated with human trafficking: An updated systematic review. *Epidemiology and Psychiatric Sciences, 25*(4), 317–341.

Pew Research Center. (2020). *Many Black and Asian Americans say they have experienced discrimination amid the COVID-19 outbreak.* https://www.pewsocialtrends.org/2020/07/01/many-black-and-asian-americans-say-they-have-experienced-discrimination-amid-the-covid-19-outbreak/

Polaris. (2022, January). *Human trafficking trends in 2020: An analysis of data from the U.S. National Human Trafficking Hotline.* https://polarisproject.org/wp-content/uploads/2022/01/Human-Trafficking-Trends-in-2020-by-Polaris.pdf

Polaris. (2019, September). *The typology of modern slavery defining sex and labor trafficking in the United States.* https://polarisproject.org/wp-content/uploads/2019/09/Polaris-Typology-of-Modern-Slavery-1.pdf

Powell, C., Asbill, M., Louis, E., & Stoklosa, H. (2017). Identifying gaps in human trafficking mental health service provision. *Journal of Human Trafficking, 4*(3), 256–269. https://doi.org/10.1080/23322705.2017.1362936

Rafferty, Y. (2018). Mental health services as a vital component of psychosocial recovery for victims of child trafficking for commercial sexual exploitation. *American Journal of Orthopsychiatry, 88*(3), 249–260. https://doi-org.ezproxylocal.library.nova.edu/10.1037/ort0000268

Rajan, I., & Bryant-Davis, T. (2021). *An examination of racial minority immigrants and the trauma of human trafficking*. https://doi.org/10.1037/0000214-010.

Sabon, L. C. (2018). Force, fraud, and coercion—what do they mean? A study of victimization experiences in a new destination Latino sex trafficking network. *Feminist Criminology, 13*(5), 456–476.

Sabri, B. (2018). Perspectives on factors related to HIV risk and preventative interventions at multiple levels: A study of African immigrant women survivors of cumulative trauma. *AIDS Education and Prevention, 5*, 419. https://doi.org/10.1521/aeap.2018.30.5.419

Sanchez, R. V., & Pacquiao, D. F. (2018). An ecological approach toward prevention and care ofvictims of domestic minor sex trafficking. *Journal of Forensic Nursing, 14*(2), 98–105.

Sangalang, C. C., Becerra, D., Mitchell, F. M., Lechuga-Peña, S., Lopez, K., & Kim, I. (2019). Trauma, post-migration stress, and mental health: A comparative analysis of refugees and immigrants in the United States. *Journal of Immigrant and Minority Health, 21*(5), 909–919. https://doi.org/10.1007/s10903-018-0826-2

Sisson, A. (2018). Access to justice for undocumented female victims of sex trafficking. *Seattle Journal for Social Justice, 17*, 91.

Turner, C. M., Arayasirikul, S., & Wilson, E. C. (2021). Disparities in HIV-related risk and socioeconomic outcomes among trans women in the sex trade and effects of a targeted, anti-sex-trafficking policy. *Social Science & Medicine, 270*, N.PAG. https://doi-org.ezproxylocal.library.nova.edu/10.1016/j.socscimed.2020.113664

United Nations Office on Drugs and Crime. (2021a). *Global report on trafficking in persons 2020: Country profile North America.* https://www.unodc.org/documents/data-and-analysis/tip/2021/GLOTIP_2020_CP_North_America.pdf

United Nations Office on Drugs and Crime. (2020, January 15). *Global report on trafficking in persons 2020.* https://www.unodc.org/documents/data-andanalysis/tip/2021/GLOTiP_2020_15jan_web.pdf

United Nations Office on Drugs and Crime. (2018). *Global report on trafficking in persons 2018: North America.* https://www.unodc.org/documents/data-and-analysis/glotip/2018/GLOTIP_2018_NORTH_AMERICA.pdf

United Nations Office on Drugs and Crime. (2012). *Global report on trafficking in persons 2012.* https://www.unodc.org/documents/data-and-analysis/glotip/Trafficking_in_Persons_2012_web.pdf

United Nations Office on Drugs and Crime. (2021b). *The effects of the COVID-19 pandemic on trafficking in persons and responses to the challenges: A global study on emerging evidence.* https://www.unodc.org/documents/humantrafficking/2021/The_effects_of_the_COVID-19_pandemic_on_trafficking_in_persons.pdf

United States Citizenship and Immigration Services. (2020a, December 10). *Green card for VAWA self-petitioner.* https://www.uscis.gov/green-card/green-card-eligibility/green-card-for-vawa-self-petitioner

United States Citizenship and Immigration Services. (2020b, July 9). *Obtaining asylum status.* USCIS. https://www.uscis.gov/forms/explore-my-options/obtaining-asylum-status

United States Citizenship and Immigration Services. (2018, June 12). *Victims of criminal activity: U nonimmigrant status.* https://www.uscis.gov/humanitarian/victims-of-human-trafficking-and-other-crimes/victims-of-criminal-activity-u-nonimmigrant-status

United States Department of Homeland Security. (2010, August). *Continued presence: Temporary immigration status for victims of human trafficking.* https://www.dhs.gov/xlibrary/assets/ht-uscis-continued-presence.pdf

United States Department of Homeland Security. (2020). *T Visa law enforcement resource guide.* https://www.uscis.gov/sites/default/files/document/guides/T-Visa-Law-Enforcement-Resource-Guide.pdf

United States Department of State. (2021, June). *2021 trafficking in persons report.* https://www.state.gov/wp-content/uploads/2021/09/TIPR-GPA-upload-07222021.pdf

United States Department of State. (2020). *2020 trafficking in persons report: United States.* https://www.state.gov/reports/2020-trafficking-in-persons-report/united-states/

van Veldhuizen, T., Horselenberg, R., Landström, S., Granhag, P. A., & van Koppen, P. J. (2017). Interviewing asylum seekers: A vignette study on the questions asked to assess credibility of claims about origin and persecution. *Journal of Investigative Psychology and Offender Profiling, 14*(1), 3–22. https://doi org.ezproxylocal.library. nova.edu/10.1002/jip.1472.

Vilches Hinojosa, M., Rivas Castillo, J., & Vidal De Haymes, M. (2021). International migration in the Central and North American regions in the COVID-19 pandemic context. *Journal of Poverty, 25*(7), 582–597.

Waters, A., & Asbill, L. (2013). Reflections on cultural humility. *CYF News*. Retrieved from American Psychological Association website: https://www.apa.org/pi/families/resources/newsletter/2013/08/cultural-humility.aspx

Wylie, L., Van Meyel, R., Harder, H., Sukhera, J., Luc, C., Ganjavi, H., … Wardrop, N. (2018). Assessing trauma in a transcultural context: Challenges in mental health care with immigrants and refugees. *Public Health Reviews, 39*(1), 22. https://doi.org/10.1186/s40985-018-0102-y

Zadnik, E., Sabina, C., & Cuevas, C. A. (2016). Violence against Latinas: The effects of undocumented status on rates of victimization and help-seeking. *Journal of Interpersonal Violence, 31*(6), 1141–1153. https://doi-org.ezproxylocal.library.nova.edu/10.1177/0886260514564062

Zhang, S. X., Pacheco-McEvoy, R., & Campos, R. (2012). Sex trafficking in Latin America: Dominant discourse, empirical paucity, and promising research. *Global Crime, 13*(1), 22–41.

# Index





J. Davidtz et al., *Sex Trafficking*, SpringerBriefs in Psychology,
https://doi.org/10.1007/978-3-031-09120-9

**T**



**V**

Made in the USA
Monee, IL
09 April 2026

48038534R00070